400+BIBLICAL LIMERICKS

Jack Malchose

WESTBOW
PRESS®
A DIVISION OF THOMAS NELSON
& ZONDERVAN

WestBow Press books may be ordered through booksellers or by contacting:

WestBow Press
A Division of Thomas Nelson & Zondervan
1663 Liberty Drive
Bloomington, IN 47403
www.westbowpress.com
844-714-3454

Scripture taken from the King James Version of the Bible.

Scripture quotations are] from the Revised Standard Version of the Bible, copyright ©
1946, 1952, and 1971 the Division of Christian Education of the National Council of the
Churches of Christ in the United States of America. Used by permission. All rights reserved.

ISBN: 978-1-6642-3842-8 (sc)
ISBN: 978-1-6642-3841-1 (hc)
ISBN: 978-1-6642-3843-5 (e)

Library of Congress Control Number: 2021913066

Print information available on the last page.

WestBow Press rev. date: 7/8/2021

PREFACE

Limericks have a bad reputation because they have developed over time a lascivious and or erotic demeanor. The most well-known author of the 'limerick' during the 19th century was the Englishman Edward Lear who was also the author of "The Owl and the Pussycat." His limericks were not like what we call limericks today because he used the same word to end both the first and fifth line of the poem. It is rather easy to find two words that rhyme but somewhat more difficult finding three. One might compose a dozen limericks in an hour using Lear's method but only two using the modern process. For instance, we find in Lear's "The Book of Nonsense" a typical example:

> There was an Old Man in a pew,
> Whose waistcoat was spotted with blue;
> But he tore it in pieces
> To give to his nieces,
> That cheerful Old Man in a pew.

A limerick has been described by some anonymous poet:

> The limerick packs laughs anatomical
> Into space that is quite economical
> But the good ones I've seen
> So seldom are clean
> And the clean ones so seldom are comical

Although Lear may have popularized the limerick, other famous authors have also tried their hand in the endeavor such as Rudyard Kipling, Mark Twain, and Louis Carroll. Even Longfellow may have used the limerick form when he wrote:

> . . . sail on, O Ship of State
> Sail on, O UNION, strong and great!
> Humanity with all its fears,
> With all the hopes of future years,
> Is hanging breathless on thy fate.

Because clean limericks are usually not comical few are composed. And for that reason, no one, to my knowledge, has written limericks with the Bible as its subject. Poetry, yes. Limericks? No. Therefore, I have assumed the task of trying to create limericks with a Biblical base and only accidentally composing some with a modicum of wit.

The Holy Bible is a best-selling book in many countries of the world. It is published in a multitude of languages and in different forms. There is a Hebrew Bible, as well as Catholic and Baptist versions. Baptists perform their baptisms by immersing the subject in water while Presbyterians dab water on the forehead with three fingers. Catholics pour a tablespoon of Holy Water on the forehead of the baptized. Although I know of no sect or denomination that bases its belief on what happened in Sodom before the conflagration (who knows?) or what transpired between a drunken Noah and his son Ham (lots of guesses), there are many verses in the Bible that can be interpreted in a plethora of ways, and this author has left the interpretation to the authors of the various editions.

The limericks in this collection are based on verses from the King James Version of the Bible, and other ancient texts, and any errors or misinterpretations are accidental and unintentional.

The Bible's a best-selling book
It appears wherever you look
In hotels it's found
By guests homeward bound
I wonder how many they took

Five books are the Torah for a Jew
The New Testament they tend to eschew,
And most of their rules
Are taught in their schools
Where they also teach children Hebrew

OLD
TESTAMENT

CHAPTER I

GENESIS

Whoever authored the book of Genesis was not a witness to the events described therein. He, whether Moses or another, used as sources myths, legends, and folktales that were circulating at the time of the author's life. An ancient proverb states that 'a myth is a bridge to the truth' so each reader of the Bible must determine what he/she believes to be the truth.

This author did not attempt to hide his belief in the existence of men before Adam or the occurrence of monumental floods around 2348 B.C.E. affecting numerous communities along river valleys from China to Egypt.

This work is not a critique of the Bible for there are many of those available to the Biblical scholar.

This is a book of limericks.

Genesis 1: 1: In the beginning God created the heavens and earth (The Big Bang, 13 billion years ago)

> There once was a very small dot.
> For a while it held quite a lot

Galaxies and stars,
Jupiter and Mars.
That dot was exceedingly hot.

Back when this whole thing began
An explosion was gargantuan.
I wasn't near it,
No one could hear it
Except God, made in the image of man

The Bible tells a similar story
It was God in all of his glory
Who created the world
And the heavens unfurled
So the universe is God's territory

Genesis 1: 3: And God said, Let there be light: and there was light.

The sun and the moon shone so bright
That the steamy old earth had some light,
But the fumes were so thick
That you could really get sick,
But algae and ferns did all right

Genesis 1: 9: And God said, Let the waters under the heaven be gathered together unto one place, and let the dry land appear: and it was so.

When the world was very young
The continents; together they clung.
Pangaea they named it,
But nobody claimed it.
From that six continents sprung

Genesis 1: 11: And God said, Let the earth bring forth grass, the herb yielding seed, and the fruit tree yielding fruit after his kind, whose seed is within itself, upon the earth: and it was so.

> God made some trees and some grasses
> To convert all of those gases.
> Into oxygen and carbon,
> Which animals live on,
> And later, the great human masses.

Genesis 1: 12: And the earth brought forth grass, and herb yielding seed. . .

> By chance photosynthesis did appear
> I don't really know in what year,
> But chlorophyll and the sun
> Formed two out of one,
> By making carbon-dioxide disappear

Genesis 1: 14: And God said, Let there be lights in the firmament of heaven...

> When finally the fumes went away
> And the sun shone brightly all day,
> On trees and some plants,
> And beetles and ants,
> And bacteria to feed on decay.

Genesis 1: 21: And God created great whales, and every living creature that moveth, which the waters brought forth abundantly, after their kind, and every winged fowl after his kind: and God saw that it was good.

For millions of years, so it seems,
There were forests, and rivers, and streams.
And deep in the subsoil
Dead animals became oil,
While plants became coal in great seams

Genesis 1: 24: And God said, Let the earth bring forth the living creature after its kind, cattle.....and beast of the earth...

Somehow big animals did appear
Though some finally did disappear,
Like dinosaurs and cats
With teeth big as rats,
And even the giant reindeer

Genesis 1: 26: And God said, Let us make man in our image, and after our likeness: and let them have dominion over the fish of the sea, and over the fowl of the air, and over the cattle, and over all of the earth, and over every creeping thing that creepeth upon the earth.

It seems there was a double creation
And both were a minor sensation.
The first man wore no clothes,
You don't see many of those,
While the second began civilization

Genesis 1: 27: So God created man in his own image...male and female...

Just when did our old earth appear?
Bishop Ussher gave us a year,
But that was of Adam
Along with his madam.
The earth is much older I fear.

Genesis 1: 28: God said unto them, be fruitful and multiply, and replenish the earth and subdue it...

> Through evolution or God's holy grace
> We humans became a new race.
> God said to go do it
> Conquer earth and subdue it,
> Until every tribe had its place

Genesis 1: 29: And God said, Behold, I have given you every herb bearing seed, which is on the face of all the earth, and every tree, in which is the fruit of a tree yielding seed: to you it shall be for meat.

> The dress of that day was as nudist.
> I don't know which was the crudest
> Bantu or Apache,
> Viking or Comanche?
> My ancestors, I know, were the rudest.

Genesis 1: 31: And God saw everything that he had made, and behold, it was very good.

> Sometimes we people might wonder
> What spell those natives were under.
> What made the Chippewa,
> The Viking or Kiowa,
> Need to kill, pillage, and plunder?

Genesis 2: 3: And God blessed the seventh day, and sanctified it: because that in it he had rested from all his work which God created and made.

> God knew that He had to rest
> He said once a week was the best.
> So the Sabbath became

The rest-day's new name,
And Sunday is one day that is blessed

Sunday we go for the sermon
Whether Scot, Polish or German.
Then there's the Jew,
Who some Saturdays blew
The Shofar his name is Sam Berman

Exodus 35: 3: Ye shall kindle no fire throughout your habitation upon the sabbath day.

Somehow it doesn't seem right
To hire goys to turn off the light,
But the day that God blessed
Is a day we should rest,
That means no work 'til tonight.

Sometimes the text needs some explaining. If you read the text properly you will see that the man and woman in Chapter 1 are not the same as the Adam and Eve in Chapter 2, though millions of scholars over thousands of years have been myopic and see only Adam and Eve in Genesis.

Early man and woman appear in about forty thousand B.C.E. and are mentioned in Chapter 1 of Genesis, verse 28, where it says, 'And God blessed them and said unto them, Be fruitful, and multiply, and replenish the earth, and subdue it…..'

The pre-Adamites were naked hunter and gatherers with no permanent address. These pre-Adamites included; the Australian aborigines, Caribbean Caribs, the African Bantus, and the Germanic Visigoths. The explorers Columbus and Cook, Burton and Speke, and Livingstone and Stanley met many of them.

Today, thanks to missionaries with their pretty colored fabrics, few pre-Adamites outside of the Amazon jungles eschew clothing and other artifacts of civilization. These South Americans are content in their gardens of Eden and are not haunted by addiction to alcohol or drugs (except for a stimulant found in coca leaves, and, if civilization encroaches upon them with its intoxicants.).

While the Christians, Muslims and Jews worship in various ways, how and when they observe their sabbath is one area in which many differ. It was God who rested after 6 days of hard work: imagine how you would feel after creating billions of galaxies, stars, and planets, not to mention plants, animals and humans. It was God's day of rest but we humans, because it was sanctified, adopted it as our day of rest. Many Christians mow their lawns on Sunday afternoon while some Jews won't pick up a dropped book because it takes work to retrieve it. God bless them all.

Genesis 2: 5: And every plant of the field before it was in the earth, and every herb of the field before it grew: for the Lord had not caused it to rain upon the earth, and there was not a man to till the ground.

> And there was no real cultivation
> What's now known as civilization,
> No plants of the field
> To provide greater yield
> Than those God made at creation.

Genesis. 2: 7 And the Lord God formed man of the dust of the ground.... and man became a living soul.

> Then from nowhere there soon appeared
> A man with no clothes and no beard.
> He was all alone

Out there on his own,
Neither animal or man interfered.

*Genesis 2: 8 : And the Lord God planted a garden eastward in Eden,
and there he put the man whom he had formed.*

At first this new man had it made,
But God was a little afraid
That Adam might wander
Among those over yonder,
So in a garden is where Adam stayed.

By calculating the ages and begats in Genesis 5, we, and Arch-Bishop Ussher of Ireland, can conclude that Adam and Eve appear around 4004 B.C.E., at about the same time as the Sumerians who came from the mountains, or the sea, or the desert, and used a language with no known relationship to any other language, and who were responsible for the domestication of plants and animals, inventing the wheel and writing, cities, and clocks.

It can be noted that the plants and animals of Chapter One's creation were 'of the earth' whereas the plants and animals in Chapter two are 'of the field'. This may or may not indicate that after Adam, or sometime after 4000 BCE, plant and animal domestication took place.

The man, Adam, was assigned to the Eden ghetto shortly after he was formed. He never got to 'replenish the earth and subdue it', as the pre-Adamites did.

If we were to list the societies that contributed the most to civilization at its beginning, topping the list would be Sumer in Mesopotamia and China in the Far East. The Sumerian innovations include the wheel, the chariot, animal domestication, the plow, irrigation, plant cultivation, writing, etc., and China is credited with bringing to light paper and printing, the compass and gunpowder, kiln-dried bricks and porcelain. Descendants of the mythical Adam may have been the intellectuals of Sumer and those of the mythical Cain may have settled in China.

Genesis 2: 9: And out of the ground made the Lord God to grow every tree that is pleasant to the sight, and good for food; the tree of life also in the midst of the garden, and the tree of knowledge of good and evil.

> This Adam, and Eve his young wife
> Had an existence that seemed free of strife.
> But they weren't very bright
> They realized in hindsight,
> They should have sampled the tree of life.

Genesis 2: 10: And a river went out of Eden to water the garden; and from thence was it parted, and came into four heads.

> Four rivers out of Eden we're told
> And one is loaded with gold,
> And some Onyx stone
> We'd like to own,
> And Bdellium has value when sold.

> In the Garden that God did prepare
> He told the new man to take care
> Of the trees and the fruit
> And moisten each root
> With water from rivers found there.

Genesis 2: 16-17: And the Lord God commanded the man, saying, Of every tree of the garden thou mayest freely eat: But of the tree of the knowledge of good and evil, thou shalt not eat of it: for in the day that thou eatest thereof thou shalt surely die.

> Then supposedly God made a rule
> Which to us might seem rather cruel.
> Of all of the trees
> One, he decrees,
> Could only be used as a fuel.

Genesis 2: 22: And the rib, which the Lord God had taken from the man, he made into a woman, and brought her unto the man.

> Since the man in the garden was alone
> God removed from his side a small bone,
> And fashioned a pal,
> A naked young gal
> Who, except being a she, was a clone

Genesis 3: 4-5: And the serpent said unto the woman, Ye shall not surely die: For God doth know that in the day ye eat thereof, then your eyes shall be opened, and ye shall be as gods, knowing good and evil.

> And who should the couple then meet?
> A snake with four legs and four feet.
> He was not on the level
> Nor was he the devil,
> But he told them what they could eat.

Genesis 3: 6 : And when the woman saw that the tree was good for food, and that it was pleasant to the eyes, and a tree to be desired to make one wise, she took of the fruit thereof, and did eat, and gave also unto her husband with her;...

God said "Eat that fruit and you'll die"
But the snake said, "Give it a try."
Adam and Eve took a bite
And found it all right,
But they, thus, God's law, did defy

Genesis 3:7: And the eyes of both of them were opened, and they knew that they were naked: and they sewed fig leaves together, and made themselves aprons.

Just like the Gods, Adam had
The knowledge of good and of bad.
He was naked he knew,
Out of sight he withdrew.
Of fig leaves he shortly was clad.

Genesis 3: 17, 19: And unto Adam he said, Because thou hast harkened unto the voice of thy wife…cursed is the ground for thy sake….In the sweat of thy face shalt thou eat bread,

East of Eden Adam had to labor.
He couldn't count on his neighbor.
They didn't know how
To plant or to plow,
So Adam did mankind a great favor

Genesis 3: 21: Unto Adam also and to his wife did the Lord God make coats of skins, and clothed them.

Somewhere in the vicinity of Eden
The Lord God found an animal feed'n.
So neat as a pin
He removed enough skin
For coats that the two would be need'n.

It was about the same time that the priest-author mentioned that God had not caused it to rain upon the earth that the verdant Sahara savannah began to dry up forming the Sahara Desert. I would suppose that the Arabian desert, as well as other deserts at that latitude would also have begun forming. Is it possible that a super-nova in the constellation of Vela around 6000 years ago may have led to the desiccation of the afore-mentioned deserts? In any case there may have been no rain at that time in those locations.

One would be hard pressed to find a mural or carving from ancient Sumer, Egypt or China that showed humans less than properly dressed. The story of Adam and Eve attempts to explain that phenomena. While the rest of the world, with the possible exception of the inhabitants of the frigid regions, was living in the fashion of the animals, copying them in many ways, including living in caves without any clothes, and hunting and gathering for their food supply, Adam and his Sumerian friends were busy building and planting, and shearing and inventing.

Adam and his descendants, and some with whom they came in contact, fashioned garments of linen, wool, or skins. Adam and his wife not only possessed the knowledge of right and wrong (a conscience) but a certain degree of modesty. Six thousand years ago God, an excellent tailor, killed some animal and made beautiful garments for his favorite couple.

Genesis 3: 23: Therefore the Lord God sent him forth from the garden of Eden, to till the ground from whence he was taken.

> Adam invented a crude little plow,
> And by the sweat of his Sumerian brow,
> He planted some seed
> As much as he'd need,
> And tamed the auroch (wild cow).

Genesis 3: 16: Unto the woman he said, I will greatly multiply thy sorrow and thy conception; in sorrow thou shalt bring forth children; and thy desire shall be to thy husband, and he shall rule over thee.

Adam knew Eve and she bore
Two boys and maybe some more.
She experienced some pain
Birthing Abel and Cain,
As God had cursed her before.

Genesis 4: 3-4: And in process of time it came to pass, that Cain brought of the fruit of the ground an offering unto the Lord. And Abel, he also brought of the firstlings of his flock and of the fat thereof.

And Cain sacrificed to his God,
Bringing grain which seems rather odd,
For gods do prefer
Offerings covered in fur,
Like lambs and calves; or fresh cod.

Genesis 4: 4: And the Lord had respect unto Abel and to his offering:

So Abel who tended the flock
Brought a lamb to the old chopping-block.
And God saw that Abel
Had brought to His table
The best of his well-cared-for stock.

Genesis 4: 8: And Cain talked with Abel his brother: and it came to pass, when they were in the field, that Cain rose up against Abel his brother, and slew him.

Now Cain was extremely upset.
He took action he soon would regret.

He upset his mother
By killing his brother,
A crime Cain would never forget.

Genesis 4: 15: And the Lord said unto him, Therefore whosoever slayeth Cain, vengeance shall be taken on him sevenfold. And the Lord set a mark upon Cain, lest any finding him should kill him.

So Cain was given a mark
Did his skin shine like a shark?
Grow horns on his head?
As somebody said
Or did he glow in the dark?

Genesis 4: 16: And Cain went out from the presence of the Lord, and dwelt in the land of Nod, on the east of Eden.

Eastward Cain had to go.
How far we really don't know.
But wherever he went
In the great Orient,
He had that strange marking to show.

Genesis 5: 8: And all the days of Seth were nine hundred and twelve years: and he died

Then Seth became boy number three
Who lived hundreds of years you'll agree.
And probably his wife
Lived a very long life.
She's not named in the Good Book you see.

Genesis 5: 7: And Seth lived after he begat Enos eight hundred and seven years, and begat sons and daughters

Seth's descendants are varied and many.
In some nations today there aren't any.
But Israelites and Jews,
Israelis and Hebrews.
The Bible doesn't mention Jack Benny.

Genesis 5: 24: And Enoch walked with God: and he was not; for God took him.

God talked with men quite a lot.
Most who walked with Him, I forgot.
It may seem rather odd
But don't walk with God,
Enoch did, and then he was not.

Genesis 18: 32: And he said, Oh let not the Lord be angry, and I will speak yet this once: Peradventure ten shall be found there. And he said, I will not destroy it for ten's sake.

God was looking for good men.
In Sodom he didn't find even ten.
What would God do
If He found twenty two?
Yes. What would He have done then?

Cain and Abel were siblings of uncertain ages. To make sure supplicants brought only animals without blemishes (since it would be natural for a parishioner to bring a lame or deformed animal to be sacrificed) the priests who wrote Chapter 2, indicated what sacrifices God preferred since they, the priests, favored lamb chops and veal cutlets.

Cain most likely possessed a conscience but it did not prevent him from committing homicide. He felt guilt but thought his punishment was greater than he could bear. He was also afraid that the primitive pre-Adamites living in the Orient might kill him. How any mark would deter others from killing him is not explained in this myth but maybe God also talked with the inhabitants of Asia.

By the seventh century B.C.E. the authors probably had seen Asians and since Cain had traveled to the East they may have thought the mark of Cain was not horns but the epicanthic fold, which many modern scientists assume evolved over centuries when the Asian man lived among the snow-covered valleys and mountains of the Himalayas. The third son of Adam and Eve was Seth who was the first among 13 mentioned descendants of Adam. They all had wives and daughters but these ladies remain nameless.

Genesis 6: 2: That the sons of God saw the daughters of men that they were fair; and they took them wives of all which they chose

> Now the sons of God, or of Adam,
> Met pretty girls and they had'em,
> As a friend or a mate
> Or just for a date,
> But I guess God hadn't forbad'em.

Genesis 6: 4 There were giants in the earth in those days; and also after that

> The sons of God were not very tall
> In fact I would say they were small
> The primitive women
> Who bedazzled the men
> Descended from giants after all

Genesis. 6: 4: ....when the sons of God came in unto the daughters of men, and they bore children to them, the same became mighty men which were of old, men of renown.

Of these unions children were born
Who grew as tall as the corn.
Some were renown
Known up and down,
But others brought only scorn.

Genesis 6: 5: And god saw that the wickedness of men was great in the earth, and that every imagination of the thoughts of his heart was only evil continually.

When God saw the evil in men
He decided right there and then,
To destroy the whole lot
But just then he thought,
I'll save a few men and their women.

It turns out that not many had
A conscience; that's very sad.
Every sin they'd devise
Was enormous in size,
And robbery and murder, egad

Genesis 6: 12 : And God looked upon the earth, and, behold, it was corrupt, for all flesh had corrupted his way upon the earth.

The primitive people you'll agree
Had no conscience like you or like me.
They didn't know right
From wrong as you might.
They were evil as evil can be

Genesis 6: 8: But Noah found grace in the eyes of the Lord

> God selected old Noah because
> Perfect in his generations he was:
> And he also was just
> Not troubled by lust.
> And this was before they wrote laws.

Genesis 6: 14: Make thee an ark of gopher wood; rooms shalt thou make in the ark, and shalt pitch it within and without with pitch.

> Now Noah was not a great sailor,
> Nor a baker or even a tailor.
> God found him the best
> Of all of the rest
> And gave him a job as a nailer.

Genesis 6: 15 : And this is the fashion which thou shalt make it: The length of the ark shall be three hundred cubits, the breadth of it fifty cubits, and the height of it thirty cubits.

> So God gave Noah the plans
> And with his very own hands
> Like a big Cutty Sark
> Noah fashioned an ark,
> Before God flooded the lands

Genesis 7: 7: And Noah went in, and his sons, and his wife, and his sons' wives with him, into the ark, because of the waters of the flood.

> In order to save several lives
> Noah took his wife, sons and their wives.
> Following beasts they all entered

A door that was centered,
To make sure that his family survives.

As the descendants of Adam moved into lands occupied by indigenous tribes they found women who were statuesque and handsome. These Adamites married, if you can call it that, as many as they chose. If the natives were not polygamous at the time, they were introduced to it by the new invaders. If there is a gene for 'conscience' this is where it first became diluted.

Some of those without a conscience saw the wealth and finery of the sons of Adam and took advantage of it. Theft, murder, rape, and violence became commonplace and God noticed. He would destroy everybody, and everything on the face of the earth. But one man, Noah, seemed without sin and worthy of exemption. In some manner God drew up a blueprint for a large floating object called an ark. And Noah set out to build one

Genesis 7: 6 : And Noah was six hundred years old when the flood of waters was upon the earth...

Noah to his family was devoted,
And as long as the big ark still floated
They had to be fed
So he baked up some bread
And several clean animals he smoted.

Genesis 5: 26-27: And Methuselah lived after he begat Lamech seven hundred eighty and two years, and he begat sons and daughters. And all the days of Methuselah were nine hundred sixty and nine years: and he died.

The Good Book does not record
If Noah took Methuselah on board.

The rains did appear
In his 969th year,
Then he went to be with his Lord.

Genesis 7: 12, 24: And the rain was upon the earth forty days and forty nights. . . . And the waters prevailed upon the earth an hundred and fifty days.

The rain covered earth in a haze
About a hundred and fifty wet days.
But it could have been more
When Noah opened the door,
And freed all the livestock to graze.

The redactor took Noah at his word.
For weeks Noah's family endured.
As from heaven it rained
But no one complained
Tho this was the first thunder they'd heard.

Genesis 7: 19: And the waters prevailed exceedingly upon the earth; and all the high hills, that were under the whole heaven, were covered.

In 2348 more than one nation
Knew nothing of precipitation.
Thunder was unheard of
Then when clouds formed above
They produced the great inundation.

In Mesopotamia floods covered the mountain.
In China it was like an overflowing fountain.
What covers a hill?
Say what you will
Eighty feet, 25000 feet, who's count'in?

Genesis 8: 3: And the waters returned from off the earth continually: and after the end of the hundred and fifty days the waters were abated.

> In China and India it took 150 years,
> But for Noah's family, those dears
> 150 days, someone wrote
> They stayed on the boat
> And then the bright sun reappears.

Genesis 9: 13: I do set my bow in the cloud, and it shall be for a token of a covenant between me and the earth.

> And finally when the flood had abated
> God then quite frequently stated,
> He'd make a deal
> And then would reveal
> A Rainbow that He had created.

Genesis 9: 14: And it shall come to pass, when I bring a cloud over the earth, that the bow shall be seen in the cloud:

> Today rain in Iraq is quite rare.
> Once they had none over there.
> No dark thunder-cloud
> To startle the crowd,
> And no rainbow to color the air.

> Noah and his family didn't know
> Since they'd never seen a rainbow,
> That way down south
> And at the Zambezi's mouth
> Man often enjoyed a colorful show.

Were there rainbows on earth before God made a covenant with Noah and his progeny that He would never again bring flood to the earth to destroy all of his landlocked creation? Certainly there were but Noah never saw them before nor did many inhabitants of the world at that latitude.

For 1658 years, while the Sahara was converting from a lush savannah to a desolate desert, no clouds appeared above Northern Africa, the Arabian Peninsula, Southern Iraq or parts of India. Then on or about 2348 BCE, by word of God or because of Climate Change, mountain glaciers began to melt, rains began to fall, and the sea level began to rise. Extensive flooding forced people to abandon their riverside villages and towns.

It has been suggested that when the Sahara was drying up and transforming from Savanna to Desert there was no summer nor winter. This is because:

(1) the early Babylonians and the Egyptians claimed twelve hours of daylight and twelve hours of darkness.

Also,
(2) the empires of the Near East used a lunar calendar rather than our more logical solar calendar.

In addition,
(3) the Sphinx temple (@2500 BCE) is aligned with the southern base of the pyramid of Khafre where the sun once set during the Equinox every day of the year. No wonder the east and west sides of the structure point so perfectly to the true north.

After 2348 BCE, the year of Noah's flood,
(4) a new Egyptian god, Horus the child, replaces the old god Horus the Elder.

Then there was the Indian storm god Indra,
(5) who is praised in the Rig Veda as: "Not even all the gathered gods conquered thee, Indra, in the war, when thou didst lengthen day into night (Rig Veda Book IV, XXX,3).

(6) Enlil, a Mesopotamian storm god, created summer and winter according to the translation by Samuel Noah Kramer in "The Tablets of Sumer" (Falcon Wing Press, 1956, Indian Hills, Colo., pg. 161) where he writes, 'Enlil, the air god, has set his mind on bringing all sorts of tree and grain, and establishing abundance and prosperity in the land. For this purpose, two cultural beings, the brothers Emesh (summer) and Enten (winter) are created, and Enlil assigned to each his specific duties.'

Then
(7) there was William Whiston, born in 1667, who published "New Theory of the Earth" and claimed that the comet of 1682 (Halley's) had a periodic of 575 years and calculated that the comet had met the earth in 2346 B.C. and caused the deluge. Further research led him to believe that before the deluge the planes of daily rotation and yearly revolution coincided and because of this there were no seasons.

Over in Mesopotamia, Noah builds a boat to God's specifications, and finally marvels at the sight of a rainbow.

Genesis 9: 20-21: And Noah began to be an husbandman, and he planted a vineyard: And he drank of the wine, and was drunken; and he was uncovered within his tent....

> So Noah got drunk and passed out.
> His son Ham evidently found out.
> He told both his brothers

But not any others.
I don't know what that's all about.

Genesis 9: 24-25: And Noah awoke from his wine, and knew what his younger son had done unto him. And he said, Cursed be Canaan; a servant of servants shall he be unto his brethren.

When Noah woke he was mad.
He figured that Ham had been bad.
So Canaan was cursed
In a silly outburst
And sons pay for sins of their dad.

Ancient Near Eastern Texts, Prichard, Princeton University Press, 1955, "Sargon, the mighty king, king of Agade, am I.....The brothers of my father loved the hills." 119.

The culture of Sumer was destroyed
But Semites appeared overjoyed.
They swooped right on down
From each mountain town,
Tho Sumerian writing was employed

Genesis 10: 8,10 : And Cush begat Nimrod: he began to be a mighty one . . . And the beginning of his kingdom was Babel, and Erech, and Accad, and Calneh. . .
Ancient Near Eastern Texts. Prichard,
"For four and (…) years I excised kingship. The black-haired people I ruled, I governed; Mighty mountains with chip-axes of bronze I conquered."

It seems that after the flood
Mesopotamia was covered with mud.
But from Accad there came

The man Sargon by name
Who conquered without spilling blood.

Genesis 11: 4: And they said, Go to, let us build us a city and a tower, whose top may reach unto heaven; and let us make us a name, lest we be scattered abroad upon the face of the whole earth.

Some Semites were men of renown
Who not only built them a town
But a tower so high
That it reached to the sky,
But then God had it all shut down.

It seems reasonable that a great flood plain like that of the land between the rivers Euphrates and Tigris would have been stripped clean of trees, villages, crops, animals and humans after a devastating flood, and after a reasonable period of time mountain tribes and desert nomads would find this territory ripe for occupation.

The Sumerians would be found at the bottom of the Persian Gulf or crawling on the beaches of the Arabian Peninsula with evidence of their landholdings floating away.

Glaciers in the passes of the Taurus and Zagros mountains melted, contributing to the flood waters, and after the flood, many who had been trapped in the mountains by glaciers were able to descend into the valley, claim some land, establish a town and construct a ziggurat; or, in the case of Babel, a tower.

Of course, coming from different areas of mountain or desert they spoke different dialects of the Semitic language, and while using the Sumerian cuneiform system of writing, the use of written and spoken Sumerian declined.

Families of Sumerians or Adamites, like that of Noah, may have become the elite of the dynasties of Sargon and his sons. Thus we know more about them than their Semitic neighbors. Shem's progeny can be traced down through the ages to another blessed by his god; Abram.

Genesis 11: 1,7: And the whole earth was of one language, and of one speech. Go to, let us go down, and there confound their language, that they may not understand one another's speech.

> Tower of Babel, as it's now known,
> The Lord God did not condone.
> He had a lesson to teach
> So he garbled their speech
> Causing many a Semite to groan.
>
> But we now know what had occurred
> Immigrants had come undeterred,
> From desert and mountain
> But no one was countin'
> Maybe 24 dialects were heard.

Genesis 11: 8: So the Lord scattered them abroad from thence upon the face of all the earth: and they left off to build the city.

> We now know pre-Adamites were there.
> Of this fact not many are aware,
> But outside of Eden
> The pagans were feed'in
> On the usual hunter-gatherer fare.

Genesis 10: 31: These are the sons of Shem, after their families, after their tongues in their lands, after their nations.

Old Shem you have to admire.
For years he went on to sire
Dozens of Hebrews
And later some Jews.
It's sad he had to retire.

Genesis 11: 31: And Terah took Abram his son, and Lot the son of Haran his son's son, and Sarai his daughter in law, his son Abram's wife; and they went forth with them from Ur of the Chaldees, to go into the land of Canaan; and they came unto Haran, and dwelt there.

Why Terah and Abram left Ur
Of an answer we aren't very sure.
Was it that the Edomites attacked,
Or was it pastures they lacked,
Or God's ordering their departure?

Abram left the land of his birth
And began to travel the earth.
Up the Euphrates to Haran
Then over to Canaan.
He was able to double his worth.

Genesis 12: 1: Now the Lord had said unto Abram, Get thee out of thy country, and from thy kindred, and from thy father's house, unto a land I will show thee:

So after a lengthy and prosperous rest.
Twenty years I would have guessed.
Though Abram was old
By God he was told,
Leave for Canaan out in the west.

Genesis 12: 4: So Abram departed, as the Lord had spoken unto him; and Lot went with him: and Abram was seventy and five years ol d when he departed out of Haran.

>Surprised that Abram was so old?
>At least that's what we are told.
>And Sarai, his wife
>Also had a long life,
>And her beauty a sight to behold.

Genesis 12: 10 : And there was a famine in the land: and Abram went down into Egypt to sojourn there; for the famine was grievous in the land.

>When famine in Canaan was at hand
>Abram gathered his extensive band,
>And traveling south
>To the great Nile's mouth,
>He abandoned his God's Promised Land.

Genesis 12: 13,15: Say, I pray thee, you art my sister: that it may be well with me for thy sake; and my soul shall live because of thee.
The princes also of Pharaoh saw her, and commended her before Pharaoh: and the woman was taken into Pharaoh's house.

>When Abram said his wife was his sister
>We're not sure that he even missed her.
>She stayed with Pharaoh
>What they did I don't know
>He said he hadn't even kissed her.

Genesis 11: 30: But Sarai was barren; she had no child.

That Sarai was barren's a fact,
So they were rather slow to react
When God promised a child
They both doubtfully smiled,
'Twas belief in God's word that they lacked.

Genesis 17: 5: Neither shall thy name any more be called Abram, but thy name shall be Abraham;

If you want God to give you a name,
Make sure wrestling's your game,
Or have children I'm told
When you're ninety years old
Or if forming great nation's your aim.

Genesis 17: 15: And God said unto Abraham, As for Sarai thy wife, thou shalt not call her name Sarai, but Sarah shall her name be.

God renamed quite a few,
Most likely if you were a Jew.
Jacob was Israel now,
Abram was Abraham somehow.
I wonder, did He rename you?

Sometime after 2000 B.C.E., Abram, his wife Sarai, and his nephew Lot followed Terah, Abram's father, out of Ur, which later was in the Chaldees, up to the source of the Euphrates, and stayed a spell at Haran, where Terah died at the age of 205.

Around this time, Abram's God instructed him to take his assemblage and Lot and continue to Canaan, with His blessing. In those days God promoted the idea that a wife could give her handmaid to her husband to have children and Abram went into Hagar, the

Egyptian servant of Sarai, and she conceived and produced a child who Abram, as instructed by an angel, called Ishmael.

God made a covenant with Abram in which Abram would be the father of a great multitude and occupy Canaan. Abram and his male followers would sacrifice a useless part of their anatomy by way of a circumcision. A brisathon was planned and all males in Abraham's entourage were circumcised.

Sarai became fertile at an advanced age. Sarai conceived and was renamed Sarah while Abraham named his son, Isaac.

Genesis 19: 32: Come, let us make our father drink wine, and we will lie with him, that we may preserve seed of our father.

> There once was a fellow named Lot
> Who most of us have completely forgot.
> He fathered the Moabites,
> As well as the Amorites.
> But in Sunday school that's seldom taught.

Genesis 19: 37-38: And the first born bare a son, and called his name Moab: the same is the father of the Moabites unto this day.
And the younger, she also bore a son, and called his name Ben-ammi: the same is the father of the children of Ammon unto this day.

> The Hebrew cousins were Moabites
> And others were the Ammonites,
> But whenever they met
> You certainly could bet
> Their meetings would end up in fights,

Genesis 21: 1-3: And the Lord visited Sarah as he had said, and the Lord did unto Sarah as he had spoken. For Sarah conceived, and bare

Abraham a son in his old age, at the set time of which God had spoken to him. And Abraham called the name of his son that was born unto him, whom Sarah bare to him, Isaac.

Sarai had a boy... just the one.
At her age he wasn't much fun.
Like any other kid
He did what he did,
She wondered what she had begun.

Genesis 24: 2,4: And Abraham said unto his eldest servant of his house, that ruled over all that he had... But thou shalt go unto my country, and to my kindred, and take a wife unto my son Isaac.

Finally when Isaac was mature
That God's chosen people might endure,
A servant one day
Was sent on his way
A young wife for Isaac to procure.

Genesis 24: 51,53: Behold, Rebekah is before thee, take her, and go, and let her be thy master's son's wife, as the Lord hath spoken. And the servant brought forth jewels of silver, and jewels of gold, and raiment, and gave them to Rebekah: he gave also to her brother and to her mother precious things.

Rebekah lived in Padan-Aram.
She descended, like Isaac, from Adam.
For jewels and gold,
I guess she was sold
To the servant of Old Abraham.

Genesis 24: 63,67: And Isaac went out to meditate in the field at the eventide: and he lifted up his eyes, and saw, and, behold, the camels were coming.
And Isaac brought her unto his mother Sarah's tent, and took Rebekah, and she became his wife, and he loved her: and Isaac was comforted after his mother's death.

> When Isaac met Rebekah in a field
> His pleasure he hardly concealed.
> To his mother he went
> To help plan an event
> Soon the marriage of Isaac was revealed.

Genesis 27: 11,16,21,23: And Jacob said to Rebekah his mother, Behold, Esau my brother is a hairy man, and I am a smooth man: and she put the skins of the kids of the goats upon his hands, and upon the smooth of his neck. And Isaac said unto Jacob, Come near, I pray thee, that I may feel thee, my son, whether thou be my very son Esau or not. And he discerned him not, because his hands were hairy, as his brother Esau's hands: so he blessed him.

> The story of Jacob and his mother
> Is not just like any other.
> They did Isaac deceive
> And thus did receive
> The blessings due Esau his brother.

Genesis 27: 41: And Esau hated Jacob because of the blessing wherewith his father blessed him: and Esau said in his heart, The days of mourning for my father are at hand; then will I slay my brother Jacob.

> Now Jacob didn't want to be killed.
> Of that he wasn't exactly thrilled.
> So he went to Haran

To stay with his clan,
Until his commitment there was fulfilled.

Genesis 29: 18,23,27: And Jacob loved Rachel; and said, I will serve thee seven years for Rachel thy younger daughter. And it came to pass in the evening, that he took Leah his daughter, and brought her to him; and he went in unto her.
Fulfill her week, and we will give thee this also for the service which thou shalt serve with me yet seven other years.

Well, deception Jacob knew very well,
Though Esau, his birthright, did sell.
Then back in Haran
His uncle Laban
Made him work for two wives quite a spell.

Genesis 33: 1: And Jacob lifted up his eyes, and looked, and, behold, Esau came, and with him four hundred men. And he divided the children unto Leah, and unto Rachel, and unto the two handmaids.

So Jacob started twelve Jewish tribes,
By maids and servants and wives.
There was Gad and Simeon,
And Dan and Zebulun.
Ultimately thousands of lives.

Many primitive tribes learned early to steal brides from neighboring tribes to help prevent certain afflictions caused by inbreeding. The Hebrews, being the chosen people, would rather keep the blood unadulterated and preferred to marry cousins than people of questionable heritage.

Although Ham was supposedly the father of Canaan and Canaan the patriarch of the territory of Canaan, one wonders if the story of a naked Noah, Ham and Canaan was written by "J" to justify the enslavement of Canaanites by the Israelites and that the Canaanite women Abraham and Isaac eliminated as brides for their sons were not descendants of Adam or Noah. While we are wondering we may as well wonder if the handmaids of Leah and Rachel were of the Adamite line. Hagar, the servant of Sarah, and mother of Ismael, was an Egyptian and could plausibly be a distant relative of Abraham. That association could help explain why Abram and the Israelites were so welcome in Egypt during the twentieth and nineteenth centuries B.C.E.

The appearance of primarily Jewish 'diseases' such as Tay-Sachs, Cystic Fibrosis, or Bloom Syndrome may have resulted from the high incidence of cousin to cousin marriages. Today, in those areas of the world where Jews enjoy equality with the gentiles, unions between gentiles and Jews are more common and acceptable and the genetic diseases mentioned above may be less prevalent.

Genesis 37: 18,21: And when they saw him afar off, even before he came near, they conspired against him to slay him. And Reuben heard it, and he delivered him out of their hands; and said, Let us not kill him.

> Joseph wasn't liked by his brothers
> Who were born of four different mothers.
> They wanted him dead,
> But Rueben instead
> Quickly overruled all of the others.

Genesis 37: 23-24: And it came to pass, when Joseph was come unto his brethren, that they stript Joseph out of his coat, his coat of many colours that was on him; and they took him, and cast him into a pit: and the pit was empty, there was no water in it.

They found a convenient pit
And put brother Joseph in it
Until a caravan came by
That wanted to buy
Any enemy, convict, or nit-wit

Genesis. 39: 1 And Joseph was brought down to Egypt; and Potiphar, an officer of Pharaoh, captain of the guard, an Egyptian, bought him of the hands of the Ishmaelites, which had brought him down thither.

In Egypt Joseph finally arrived
Fortunate to have survived.
Then Potiphar bought him
And seems to have taught him
As both appear to have thrived.

Genesis 39: 7: And it came to pass after these things, that his master's wife cast her eyes upon Joseph; and she said, Lie with me.

But Joseph's high status was brief,
Like today's Jews he wasn't the chief
And Potiphar's wife
Put strife in his life
And he ended in jail like a thief.

Genesis 41: 15: And Pharaoh said unto Joseph, I have dreamed a dream, and there is none that can interpret it: and I have heard say of thee, that thou canst understand a dream to interpret it.

But Joseph had an Ace up his sleeve.
He persuaded Pharaoh to believe
That it would seem
He could interpret a dream,
And thus a future famine did relieve.

Genesis 42: 8,25: And Joseph knew his brethren, but they knew him not. Then Joseph commanded to fill their sacks with corn, and to restore every man's money into his sack, and to give them provision for the way: and thus did he unto them.

> One day most of old Jacob's brood
> Went down to Egypt for food.
> Joseph's kin didn't know him
> But what did they owe him?
> Nothing. He was in a generous mood.

Exodus 1: 8,11: Now there rose up a new king over Egypt, which knew not Joseph. Therefore they did set over them taskmasters to afflict them with their burdens. And they built for Pharaoh treasure cities, Pithom and Ramses.

> Finally, Jacob's clan reappears
> In Egypt, ending their fears,
> Until a Pharaoh and his clerk
> Put all Jews to work
> As slaves for quite a few years.

Genesis 49: 28: All these are the twelve tribes of Israel: and this is it that their father spake unto them, and blessed them; every one according to his blessing he blessed them.

> Israel blessed Joseph before he died,
> And his brothers were also sanctified.
> There were so many
> He didn't skip any
> Cause it seems they all qualified.

Certain archaeologists have argued that pre-dynastic Egypt was influenced by travelers from the east; from Arabia and from

Mesopotamia. Cylinder seals, masonry design, and pictographic writing seem to have been borrowed from eastern civilizations.

Later Abraham, Jacob, and Joseph find, at least for a while, a friendly neighbor in Egypt. Joseph became a trusted advisor to the Pharaoh and was able to help his extended family become permanent residents of the kingdom on the Nile.

While Israel (Jacob) may have predicted great things for his offspring, he could not have known of the ten lost tribes nor the exile of the elite of Judah to Babylon, the destruction of the second temple and the distribution of Jews throughout the kingdoms of Greece and Rome.

Israel evidently did not dream of the Roman or Spanish inquisition or the expulsion of Jews from Great Britain or the Pale of Settlements or pogroms in Russia, nor Holocaust perpetrated by the Nazis in Germany.

However, in the Diaspora, whether in Europe, the Americas or Asia, a great many of Jacob's descendants married gentiles and had children who married gentiles until few Jewish genes remain. Although if you are an O'Leary or a Sanchez, you may also be among the millions of descendants of Abraham and Jacob; and you may be Catholic, Protestant, Buddhist, Muslim or atheist.

In subsequent centuries Hebrews and Jews became advisors or assistants to many emperors and leaders such as Charlemagne, but with the exception of Disraeli and a few others, they never assumed a leadership position, other than in business, until Israel became a nation.

CHAPTER 2

EXODUS

The book of Exodus concerns itself with the plans to persuade the unnamed Pharaoh of Egypt to let Moses' and God's people go. Several dozen verses in Exodus as well as Leviticus and Numbers have chapters beginning with "And the Lord spake unto Moses, saying", followed by proposals, laws, or commandments. The Lord, thereby, assisted in gaining the freedom of His people from slavery in Egypt and then provided them with the rules for living and dying, worshipping and offering, and avoiding the wrath of God.

Exodus 1: 7: And the children of Israel were fruitful, and increased abundantly, and multiplied, and waxed exceedingly mighty, and the land was filled with them.

> Well, Jacob and Joseph had died.
> To Israelites school was denied.
> In math they were bad
> They just couldn't add
> But Torah says they multiplied.

Exodus 1: 11: Therefore they did set over them taskmasters to afflict them with their burdens.

The Pharaoh then began to fear,
"We've got a big problem here,
Israelites are a scourge,
Their numbers do surge,
Let's enslaved them later this year."

Exodus 1: 15-17: And the king of Egypt spake to the Hebrew midwives…. And he said, When ye do the office of a midwife to the Hebrew women, and see them upon the stools, if it be a son, then ye shall kill him; but if it be a daughter, then she shall live. But the midwives feared God, and did not as the king of Egypt commanded them…..

Two Hebrew gals were midwives
Who should have taken some lives,
But God they did fear
They knew He was near
And that's how a midwife survives.

Exodus 2: 1-2: And there went a man of the house of Levi, and took to wife a daughter of Levi. And the woman conceived, and bare a son:

Moses was a Levite they say,
And his mother one sunny day
With pitch and bitumen
Made an ark to put him in
And in the Nile, hid him away.

Exodus 2: 16,18,21: 3: 1: Now the priest of Midian had seven daughters: And when they came to Reuel their father…… And Moses was content to dwell with the man: and he gave Moses Zipporah his daughter.
Now Moses kept the flock of Jethro his father in law, the priest of Midian…

There was a priest Jethro Reuel
Who seems to us rather cool.
He gave Moses his daughter
Cause he helped her get water
For her flock out by the pool.

Exodus 2: 24: And God heard their groaning, and God remembered his covenant with Abraham, with Isaac, and with Jacob.

God's memory, as it's portrayed,
In Egypt it once was displayed.
He heard groaning and sighing
and moaning and crying
And recalled a promise he'd made.

Exodus 4: 10: And Moses said unto the Lord. I am not eloquent, neither heretofore, nor since thou hast spoken unto thy servant: but I am slow of speech, and of a slow tongue.

Moses was Levi's grandson,
And Aaron was the other one.
Moses would stutter
Or else he would mutter
So Aaron was the spokesperson.

Leviticus 11: 1,7: And the Lord spake unto Moses and to Aaron, saying unto them. And the swine, though he divide the hoof, and be clovefooted, yet he cheweth not the cud; he is unclean to you.

The Lord spake unto Moses saying,
It may be somewhat dismaying
But I forbid you to eat
Clams or pigs feet,
And cover your head if you're praying.

Exodus 4: 11: And the Lord said unto him, who hath made man's mouth? or who maketh the dumb, or deaf, or the seeing, or the blind? have not I the Lord?

> It seems if you really can't see
> Don't hear well, like you or like me
> It is rather odd
> That a benevolent God
> Was responsible, don't you agree?

Exodus. 4: 20 And Moses took his wife and his sons, and set them upon an ass, and he returned to the land of Egypt: and Moses took the rod of God in his hand.

> Now Zipporah was rather small
> And her sons were not very tall
> But three on an ass
> Might seem to surpass
> Any records that I can recall

Exodus. 4: 21: And the Lord said unto Moses, When thou goest to return into Egypt, see that thou do all those wonders before Pharaoh, which I have put in thine hand: but I will harden his heart, that he shall not let the people go.

> Now we wonder, What's going on?
> Wasn't Moses God's favorite son?
> He said at the start
> He would harden Pharaoh's heart.
> Whose side was God really on?

Exodus 5: 7: Ye shall no more give the people straw to make brick, as heretofore: let them go gather straw for themselves.

The Israelites tried making bricks
Without putting straw in the mix.
But Pharaoh had implied
Put something inside,
Like grass or small wooden sticks.

*Exodus 6: 20: And Amram took him Jochebed his father's sister to wife,
and she bare him Aaron and Moses....*

Moses had a weird family tree,
At least it seems so to me.
His aunt was his mother
They don't list any other.
Did he call her Auntie or Mommy?

*Exodus 7:14: And the Lord said unto Moses, Pharaoh's heart is hardened,
he refuses to let the people go.*

Thieves tore his mummy apart
But saved Pharaoh's hard heart.
And you'd be dismayed,
It's proudly displayed
In an Egyptian Museum of Art.

*Exodus. 7: 20: And Moses and Aaron did so, as the Lord commanded,
and he lifted up the rod, and smote the waters that were in the river, in
the sight of Pharaoh, and in the sight of his servants; and all the waters
that were in the river were turned to blood.*

Egypt had a contest of rods.
I don't know what were the odds
But Pharaoh was undaunted
As his servants flaunted
Their magic; it was equal to God's.

Exodus 8: 6: And Aaron stretched out his hand over the waters of Egypt; and frogs came up and covered the land of Egypt.

> When Aaron extended his hand
> Frogs appeared all over the land,
> And tadpoles and worms
> And millions of germs
> Seemed to come out of the sand.

Exodus 12: 29: And it came to pass, that at midnight the Lord smote all the firstborn in the land of Egypt....

> After locusts and lice, you'd believe
> Pharaoh would let Israelites leave.
> But killing the firstborn
> Caused the people to mourn,
> And even led Pharaoh to grieve.

It took the trinity of Moses, Aaron and God about nine visits with the Pharaoh of Egypt before he was persuaded to give the enslaved Israelites their freedom and allow them to depart from Egypt to hold a feast unto the Lord. It would be called the feast of the Passover because the Lord was able to pass over the homes of the Israelites the night of the killing of the firstborn of Egypt.

Whether they left the country near Lake Timsah or The Red Sea as indicated or from the cities of Ramses or Pithom, which they had built for Pharaoh, they entered the desert and had God given instructions as to how to make unleavened bread and sacrifice unblemished lambs.

Exodus 13: 18: But God led the people about, through the way of the wilderness of the Red Sea: and the children of Israel went up harnessed out of the land of Egypt.

Exodus seems to mean 'going out',
That's what this book is about.
How Moses and the Lord
Brought the Israelite horde
From Egypt to the Sinai route.

Exodus 15: 4-5: Pharaoh's chariots and his host hath he cast into the sea: his chosen captains also are drowned in the Red sea. The depths have covered them : they sank into the bottom as a stone.

They've discovered the unsinkable Titanic
Those scientists with interests oceanic.
How hard can it be
To scour the Red sea,
And discover Egyptian things inorganic?

Exodus 15: 23: And when they came to Marah, they could not drink of the waters of Marah, for they were bitter:

Why worry if the water's not sweet
God's mission is not yet complete.
With the power of His mind
You suddenly find
Sweet water covering your feet.

Exodus 16: 12-13 At even ye shall eat flesh, and in the morning ye shall be filled with bread….And it came to pass, that at even the quails came up, and covered the camp…

Manna was the name of the bread
Without it they soon would be dead.
We never again heard
Of that quail-like bird
On which one night they were fed.

Exodus 19: 9,12: And the Lord said onto Moses, Lo, I come unto thee in a thick cloud that the people may hear when I speak with thee, and believe thee forever. And thou shalt set bounds unto the people round about, saying, Take heed to yourselves, that ye go not up to the mount, or touch the border of it:

God spoke to Moses from a cloud.
It says the message was out loud.
The people did hear it
They didn't come near it
Touching the mount is not allowed.

Exodus 20: 3,8 : Thou shalt have no other gods before me. Remember the sabbath day, to keep it holy.

Don't worship other gods before me
Says Exodus 20, Verse Three.
And thou shalt not kill
Whoever you will,
And keep the sabbath always holy.

Exodus 21: 12: He that smiteth a man, so that he die, shall be surely put to death.

In Exodus God starts to list
The rules He had previously missed.
"By slaying a slave
You'll rest in your grave.
Don't hit a man with your fist."

Exodu. 23: 10-11: And six years thou shalt sow thy land, and shalt gather in the fruits thereof: But the seventh year thou shalt let it rest and lie still; that the poor of thy people may eat: and what they leave the beasts of the field shall eat....

At least once every seven years
You'll feed all the poor that appears.
They and the beasts
Will enjoy days of feasts
T'il the harvest that year disappears.

Exodus 24: 15,18: And Moses went up into the mount, and a cloud covered the mount. And Moses went into the midst of the cloud, and gat him up into the mount: and Moses was in the mount forty days and forty nights.

Moses was invited by his God
Up a mount where others had trod.
God carved on a stone,
That Moses would own,
Actions that would be outlawed.

Exodus 25: 35 / 26: 11 / 27: 3: And there shall be a knop under two branches of the same, and a knop under two branches of the same, and a knop under two branches of.....
And thou shalt make fifty taches of brass, and put the taches into the loops,...
And thou shalt make his pans to receive his ashes, and his shovels, and his basons, and his fleshhooks, and his firepans:

God designed for Noah a boat
And probably Joseph's colored coat.
Then a job he did tackle
Was a great tabernacle,
And Moses built a temple of note.

Exodus 28: 4 : And these are the garments which they shall make; a breastplate, and an ephod, and a robe, and a bordered coat, a mitre, and a girdle:

Not only did Yahweh design
A temple that was really fine.
Tho not his main passion
He dabbled in fashion,
And inspired the Calvin Klein line.

*Exodus 29: 39-40: The one lamb thou shalt offer in the morning; and
the other lamb thou shalt offer at even: And with the one lamb a tenth
deal of flour mingled with the fourth part of an hin of beaten oil; and
the fourth part of an hin of wine for a drink offering.*

Now God was a chef unsurpassed
His knowledge of food was so vast
He said, Butcher a lamb,
But please avoid ham,
And make a tasty kosher repast.

*Exodus 30: 13: This they shall give, every one that passeth among them
that are numbered, half a shekel after the shekel of the sanctuary: (a
shekel is twenty gerahs:) and half shekel shall be the offering of the Lord.*

The Lord God made a condition
For tabernacle admission.
Pay ten silver gerahs
To the house that's Jehovah's,
Or pray for a special provision.

*Exodus 32: 1: And when the people saw that Moses delayed to come
down out of the mount, the people gathered themselves together unto
Aaron, and said unto him, Up, make us gods, which shall go before us;
for as for this Moses....we wot not what is become of him.*

Aaron didn't know what to do.
The people were angry, that's true.

So he did what he's told
Made a calf out of gold
They prayed to gods that were new.

Most scholars believe that there may have been a time, probably between 1400 and 1200 B.C.E. when the Exodus of the Jews from Egypt occurred. Some opine that a mass exodus as related in the Bible would have produced some evidence in the records of Egypt or elsewhere, but none have been discovered. Therefore, some deduce that the exodus took place gradually over a long period of time and, as such, did not constitute an event of historical importance, except to the authors of Exodus and other religious texts.

Then there are those who place Midian, where Moses took refuge, either on the shores, east or west, of the Gulf of Acaba or in Northwest Arabia. In any case, the Midianites were distant relatives of Moses; the Midianites were descended from Abraham and his second wife, Keturah.

Wherever the truth lies, the Exodus makes a good story and a pretty good movie.

CHAPTER 3

LEVITICUS

The Book of Leviticus is a barbecue guidebook for whenever you choose to make a sin offering, a peace offering or a meat offering.

Of course, since most of us have become residents of cities and no longer are shepherds or ranchers, we tend to substitute shekels for rams and lambs. A ten percent tithe may seem like a heavy burden, even for the rich, but the synagogues, cathedrals, churches and mosques require expensive maintenance and the poor have to be fed.

The lead characters in Leviticus are The Lord, Moses, and Aaron and his sons. Whether the Israelites had unbelievable memories like Saul Bellow, Steven Jay Gould or Isaac Asimov I know not, but if not, we would hope that they recorded all the instructions so that they could adhere to the commands of the Lord.

Fortunately, whether it is a burnt offering, a meat offering, or any other offering, the instructions are similar and they are repeated frequently throughout the third book.

Leviticus 2: 1,13: And when any will offer a meat offering unto the Lord, his offering shall be of fine flour; and he shall pour oil upon it, and put frankincense thereon: And every oblation of thy meat offering shalt thou season with salt......with all thine offerings thou shalt offer salt.

> The Torah is specific about condiments,
> So after cutting the meat into segments
> Salt and oil the meat
> Frankincense is sweet,
> And don't splash oil on your vestments.

Leviticus 4: 7 / 8: 15 / 9: 9: And the priest shall put some of the blood upon the horns of the alter... And he slew it; and Moses took the blood, and put it upon the horns of the alter....
and the sons of Aaron brought the blood to him: and he dipped his finger in the blood and put it upon the horns of the alter.

> If you plan to memorize the Torah,
> The one used in the Diaspora,
> Leviticus is neat
> Its verses repeat
> And that's even in Spanish, señora.

Leviticus 5: 7: And if he be not able to bring a lamb, then he shall bring for his trespass, which he hath committed, two turtledoves, or two young pigeons, unto the Lord; one for a sin offering, and the other for a burnt offering.

> Calves and lambs can be roasted,
> Pigeons and kids may be toasted.
> The blood or the fat
> Do not eat that.
> Other commands will be posted.

Leviticus 5: 11: But if he be not able to bring two turtlledoves, or two young pigeons, then he that sinned shall bring for his offering the tenth part of an ephah of fine flour for a sin offering;

> For a sacrifice you should be prepared.
> Skip animals even slightly impaired
> If you don't have a ram
> Or even a lamb,
> Bring a handful of flour that can be spared.

Leviticus 7: 9: And all the meat offering that is baken in the oven, and all that is dressed in the fryingpan, and in the pan, shall be the priest's that offereth it.

> If it's goat or lamb that you offer,
> Or maybe a pigeon you proffer,
> Priests prefer meat
> But if you're discreet,
> You may add two coins to the coffer.

Leviticus 8: 7-8: And he put upon him the coat, and girded him with the girdle, and clothed him with the robe, and put the ephod upon him, and he girded him with the curious girdle of the ephod...
And he put the breastplate upon him; also he put in the breastplate the Urim and the Thummim.

> If a priest has no Ephod with him
> He may substitute instead a Urim.
> As any breastplate
> Would seem second-rate,
> Without both a Urim and a Thummim.

Leviticus 10: 1-2: And Nadab and Abihu, the sons of Aaron, took either of them his censer, and put fire therein, and put incense thereon, and offered strange fire before the Lord, which he commanded them not. And there went out fire from the Lord and devoured them, and they died before the Lord.

> One way to engender the Lord's ire
> Is to offer up a strange fire.
> Like Nadab and Abihu
> You could go too,
> If that's the good Lord's desire.

Leviticus 11: 7: And the swine, though he divide the hoof, and be clovenfooted, yet he cheweth not the cud; he is unclean to you.

> The name Seth is common to Jews,
> It's a name they quite frequently use.
> But naming modern kids
> What the good Lord forbids
> Means Ham they're not likely to choose.

Leviticus 11: 13, 19, 22: And these are they which…shall not be eaten… the eagle, and the ossifrage, and the ospray. And the stork, and the heron….., and the lapwing, and the bat. Even these of them ye may eat; the locust….., and the bald locust….., and the beetle…., and the grasshopper after his kind.

> Do not eat the eagle or eaglet
> And the heron you can forget.
> Then there's the bat
> You cannot eat tha.
> Try a beetle covered in chocolate.

Leviticus 12: 3: And on the eighth day the flesh of his foreskin shall be circumcised.

> A ceremony Jews call a bris
> Seems to go something like this.
> If your bundle of joy
> Is a cute baby boy
> A rabbi removes what baby won't miss.

Leviticus 13: 2: When a man shall have in the skin of his flesh a rising, a scab, or bright spot, and it be in the skin of his flesh like the plague of leprosy; then he shall be brought unto Aaron the priest, or unto one of his sons the priests:

> Oh, back in the good olden days,
> Before the barber-as-surgeon craze,
> The doctors were Levites
> Priests of the Israelites
> Who could treat almost any malaise.

Leviticus 13: 9: When the plague of leprosy is in a man, then he shall be brought unto the priest;

> Heart disease and cancer may have been
> Well known diseases way back then.
> Leprosy, I'm sure,
> Tho they had a cure,
> Was the disease feared by most men.

The first five books of the Torah (the Pentateuch) have been attributed to Moses but he may have been assisted by other members of the tribe of Levi. Leviticus, as the name implies, is mainly devoted to the welfare of Moses, Aaron, and the priests of the Levite community.

The populace were instructed to bring their sacrifices to the Lord, but as the Lord ate sparingly, most of the flesh, fowl and foodstuff was used to nourish the priests and the poor. Even if the people killed a beast away from the vicinity of the tabernacle, a portion was claimed by the Lord and the killer would suffer the penalty of death should this requirement not be met.

Subsequently, the Tabernacle was replaced by the Temple where animals continued to be sacrificed to the Lord. The Temple and its priests were replaced by the Synagogue with its rabbinate where the sacrifice of animals was replaced by monetary donations to the Lord, through the synagogue's treasury. Today, where it has not been abolished, tithing - giving a tenth of one's income to the Lord - is common among Jews, Catholics, and Protestants.

Leviticus 14: 5-7: And the priest shall command that one of the birds be killed in an earthen vessel over running water….
And shall dip the living bird in the blood of the bird that was killed….
And he shall sprinkle upon him that is to be cleansed from the leprosy seven times, and shall pronounce him clean….

> Leprosy's not as bad as we've heard
> Moses knew how it could be cured.
> He frequently said
> On your bed or your head,
> Seven times sprinkle blood of a bird.

Leviticus 15: 7: And he that toucheth the flesh of him that hath the issue shall wash his clothes, and bathe himself in water, and be unclean until the even.

> We know God's word to be true
> So the following might likely ensue.
> Anyone who hath

A need of a bath
Should be kissed by one with an issue.

Leviticus 16: 4: He shall put on the holy linen coat, and he shall have the linen breeches upon his flesh, and shall be girded with a linen girdle, and with the linen mitre shall be attired: these are holy garments; . . .

The people grew grapes and wheat
And flax and enough food to eat.
And Aaron was admired
For he was attired
In linen from his head to his feet.

Leviticus 16: 10, 2, But the goat, on which the lot fell to be the scapegoat, shall be presented alive before the Lord, to make an atonement with him, and to let him go for a scapegoat into the wilderness.
And Aaron shall lay both his hands upon the head of the live goat, and confess over him all the iniquities of the children of Israel, and all their transgressions in all their sins, putting them on the head of the goat, and shall send him away by the hand of a fit man into the wilderness.

The word Scapegoat is very old
For in Leviticus 16 we are told,
Aaron put the sin
Of all of his kin
On a scapegoat he freed, rather than sold.

Leviticus 17: 3: What man soever there be of the house of Israel, that killeth an ox, or lamb, or goat, in the camp, or that killeth it out of the camp, And bringeth it not unto the door of the tabernacle of the congregation, to offer an offering unto the Lord before the tabernacle of the Lord; blood shall be imputed unto that man; he hath shed blood; and that man shall be cut off from among his people.

The Levite priests have to eat.
They like bread, and fowl and fresh meat.
So if you kill a beast
And are planning a feast,
Be sure the Lord's mandates you meet.

Leviticus 18: 29: For whosoever shall commit any of these abominations, even the souls that commit them shall be cut off from among their people.

Abominations upset the Lord
There are dozens he has deplored.
Ham didn't uncover,
But he did discover,
Noah's nakedness, as they record.

Leviticus 19: 5-6: And if ye offer a sacrifice of peace offerings unto the Lord, ye shall offer it at your own will.
It shall be eaten the same day ye offer it, and on the morrow; and if ought remain until the third day, it shall be burnt in the fire

On leftovers the Lord was precise,
Next day it is still very nice
But on the third day
Please burn it away
And prepare for the next sacrifice.

Leviticus. 21: 5 They shall not make baldness upon their head, neither shall they shave off the corner of their beard, nor make any cuttings in their flesh.

If you're naturally bald that's okay
Your grampa and father were that way.
But don't shave your head

Let it grow long instead,
And you won't have a barber to pay.

To live under the rules and regulations given by the Lord to Moses to relay to the multitude must have been a chore but our modern laws are probably as numerous and daunting. Only the true believers today would blame the Lord for their handicaps be they blindness, deafness, or the inability to speak. We tend to put the onus on our parents, or ancestors who possessed a similar handicap. One great fear among our generation is that we will develop Alzheimer disease or cancer because a parent was so afflicted.

Leprosy seems to have been the major affliction in the day of Moses and Aaron but God, through his human servants, has greatly reduced its occurrence and severity. A number of subsequent diseases have made their appearance and have been defeated by science while others such as Ebola, Malaria and influenza continue to present a challenge.

A few parents have blamed the Lord for the death of their child and have lost their faith. Considering all the abominations we commit we should thank the Lord for not suffering the punishments of death or being cut off from our kin.

Leviticus 21: 18 : Exodus 4: 11: For whatsoever man he be that hath a blemish, he shall not approach: a blind man, or a lame, or he that hath a flat nose, or any thing superfluous. . .
. . who maketh the dumb, or deaf, or the seeing, or the blind? have not I the Lord?

Ye with the flat nose, take note.
The priest at the temple may have wrote.
"Ye shall not come near,

I hope that is clear,
So go back home with your goat."

Leviticus 23: 33-34: And the Lord spake unto Moses, saying,
Speak unto the children of Israel, saying, The fifteenth day of this
seventh month shall be the feast of the tabernacles for seven days unto
the Lord.

One of God's numbers is seven
It probably won't get you to heaven,
But each seventh day
Is for rest or for play
And dine on bread that's unleaven.

Leviticus 24: 5-6: And thou shalt take fine flour, and bake twelve cakes
thereof: two tenth deals shall be in one cake. And thou shalt set them in
two rows, six on a row, upon the pure table before the Lord.

If you happen to like many rules
There are lots of them in our schools.
But your best bet
Is to hurry and get
A Bible with more value than jewels.

Leviticus 25: 4: But in the seventh year shall be a sabbath of rest unto
the land, a sabbath for the Lord: thou shalt neither sow thy field, nor
prune thy vineyard.

Every seven years give the land a break
Neither sow, nor prune, nor rake.
It's sabbath you see,
For field and tree
And you take a rest, for health's sake.

Leviticus 25: 44: Both thy bondmen, and thy bondmaids, which thou shalt have, shall be of the heathen that are round about you; of them shall ye buy bondmen and bondmaids.

> Today slavery is rather rare
> Though occasionally found over there.
> But in ancient days,
> As the Bible says,
> Only enslaving heathens was fair.

Leviticus 26: 20: And your strength shall be spent in vain: for your land shall not yield her increase, neither shall the trees of the land yield their fruits.

> The Lord will not give you peace
> Nor will your harvest increase,
> If His statutes you ignore
> Or His judgement abhor.
> Your strength and fame will decrease.

Leviticus 27: 32: And concerning the tithe of the herd, or of the flock, even of whatsoever passeth under the rod, the tenth shall be holy unto the Lord.

> Known to Protestant, Catholic and Jew,
> Tithing isn't a practice that's new.
> Israelites took a calf
> And cut it in half
> If their herd numbered less than a few.

The book of Leviticus, although primarily designed to guide the priests (Levites) who would be responsible for conducting or overseeing various sacrifices and ceremonies, is also aimed at the

Israelite people who are instructed, for instance, to bring unblemished animals or fowl for sacrifice.

Although God claims responsibility for the halt, lame, or blind (Exodus 4: 11) he also decrees that those with blemishes are unclean and are not to approach the alter.

God promoted good hygiene by listing a multitude of activities that would cause one to become unclean, necessitating the frequent washing, with water, of their clothes and/or their bodies to restore their cleanliness.

To provide enough water for the million Israelites there must have been a river, lake or Gulf of Aqaba in the vicinity.

CHAPTER 4

NUMBERS

The fourth book of Moses, Numbers, is appropriately named as it does provide a census of the tribes of the Israelites, at least of those males over the age of twenty.

Numbers also provides space for new instructions as to what should be brought before the Lord at the entrance to the tabernacle as a sacrifice, and for what sort of offering.

The leaders of each tribe were commanded to bring golden spoons, silver bowls, bullocks, lambs, rams, kids, oxen and he goats before the anointing of the alter. They also brought flour and oil so the million Israelites evidently did not exist solely on Manna. There was seemingly enough pasture in this part of the Sinai Peninsula - or Northwest Arabia - for the bullocks, oxen, goats and rams and enough fertile soil to produce wheat for flour and olives for oil.

Numbers also lets us know in which area the sons of Israel encamped during their forty years in the wilderness. About 35 campsites are listed as well as certain mountains such as Mount Hor where Aaron died at the age of 123. Of course, tabernacles had to be erected at each stop so that the tribes could restock the larders of the Lord. The last encampment was near the Jordan river and Jericho.

In the book of Deuteronomy ye shall read of the preparations the twelve tribes made for their taking of Canaan promised to Abraham, Isaac and Jacob.

Numbers 1: 46 / 11: 5: Even all they that were numbered were 603,550. We remember the fish, which we did eat in Egypt freely; the cucumbers, and the melons, and the leeks, and the onions, and the garlick.

> The number of numbers in Numbers
> Are likely to disturb all our slumbers.
> With thousands to feed
> They forgot to bring seed,
> So they had about zero cucumbers.

Numbers 1: 45: So were all those that were numbered of the children of Israel, by the house of their fathers, from twenty years old and upward, all that were able to go forth to war in Israel;

> Moses counted men fit for war
> Ages twenty to about fifty-four.
> Then there were plenty
> Of kids under twenty,
> And women? a half million more.

Numbers 1: 49 / 3: 2: Only thou shalt not number the tribe of Levi, neither take the sum of them among the children of Israel:
Those that were numbered of them, according to the number of all males, from a month old and upward, even those that were numbered of them were seven thousand and five hundred.

> The Lord did not think the Levites
> Should be counted like other Semites,
> So a separate poll

Included every male soul
Listing 7 thousand more Israelites.

Numbers 1: 27 / 2: 4: Those that were numbered of them, even of the tribe of Judah, were threescore and fourteen thousand and six hundred.......
And his host, and those that were numbered of them, were threescore and fourteen thousand and six hundred.

While you were reading Chapter One
You may have been blinded by the sun.
So as a special favor to you,
They repeat in Chapter two
The Census, which was well done.

Exodus 2: 15, 21: Numbers. 25: 16-17 / 31: 7:. Now when Pharaoh heard this thing, he sought to slay Moses. But Moses fled from the face of Pharaoh, and dwelt in the land of Midian: And Moses was content to dwell with the man; and he gave Moses Zipporah his daughter.

And the Lord spake unto Moses, saying, Vex the Midianites, and smite them: And they warred against the Midianites, as the Lord commanded Moses; and they slew all the males.

Now look in your Bible: the Gideon.
Moses' wife was never a Lydian.
Moses killed all her brothers
And quite a few others.
He forgot that Zipporah was a Midian.

Exodus. 4: 10 And Moses said unto the Lord, O my Lord, I am not eloquent, neither heretofore, nor since thou hast spoken unto thy servant: but I am slow of speech, and of a slow tongue.

God spake unto Moses quite a lot.
A speaker old Moses was not.
Without Aaron around
He quite often found
What he couldn't remember, he forgot.

Number 5: 7: Then they shall confess their sin which they have done: and he shall recompense his trespass with the principal thereof, and add unto it the fifth part thereof, and give it unto him against whom he hath trespassed.

Tho Israelites were almost without sin,
An occasional transpass would creep in.
Like Catholics today
They were required to pay
A fine for, say, smiting a kin.

Numbers 6: 21: This is the law of the Nazarite who hath vowed, and of his offering unto the Lord for his separation, beside that that his hand shall get: according to the vow that he vowed, so he must do after the law of his separation.

A Nazarite is an adult volunteer
Who separates themselves for a year,
Or maybe sixty weeks
If sanctity he seeks
One served forty years and that's clear.

Numbers 7: 3: And they brought their offering before the Lord, six covered wagons, and twelve oxen; a wagon for two of the princes, and for each one an ox: and they brought them before the tabernacle.

Building a tabernacle is an occasion
For planning a big celebration.

The gifts we are told
Were of silver and gold
And enough food for the next generation.

Numbers 8: 11: And Aaron shall offer the Levites before the Lord for an offering of the children of Israel, that they may execute the service of the Lord.

To this day the Levites serve the Lord
Among the chosen, they were favored.
You they will wed
And visit your sickbed
And accept what you can afford.

Numbers 9: 15: And on the day that the tabernacle was reared up the cloud covered the tabernacle, namely, the tent of the testimony: and at even there was upon the tabernacle as it were the appearance of fire, until the morning.

If the tent was covered during the day
By a cloud, or by fog, as we say.
Then at night
A fire shone bright
But by morning it all went away.

Numbers 9: 22: Or whether it were two days, or a month, or a year, that the cloud tarried upon the tabernacle, remaining thereon, the children of Israel abode in their tents, and journeyed not: but when it was taken up they journeyed.

When the fog was thick they stayed home.
When the fog lifted they could roam.
Imagine the cost

If someone got lost
That plan they use today down in Rome.

The census that Moses arranged was taken shortly after the Israelites left Egypt, and while it seems it was basically designed to determine how many mature adult men were available for combat, one can surmise that the congregation numbered over a million, counting women, children, the elderly and the disabled.

It has been suggested that if a million souls left Egypt at one short period of time, the occasion would have been noted somewhere among the vast records of ancient Egypt. Of course, if the escape of such a multitude were considered to be a defeat or failing of the pharaoh's army, the news would not have been publicized as would a victory, and Ramsses II, who may have been pharaoh at the time, erected monuments to his military successes at a multitude of points along the Nile.

Also, several Egyptologists believe that the Exodus took place over an extended period of time and would not have been considered a major event if it didn't make the evening news.

The Levites, of which Moses and Aaron were leaders, were, according to Moses, chosen by God to relay and disseminate messages from the Lord and, not surprisingly, heretofore be treated as VIPs among the gathering multitude. Those who grumbled and protested were summarily disposed of, or were threatened with elimination. Hopefully, the grumbling and protestations ceased and Moses could get on with the business of preparing for the occupation of Canaan.

Numbers 10: 2: Make the two trumpets of silver; of a whole piece shalt thou make them: that thou mayest use them for calling of the assembly, and for the journeying of the camps.

Once trumpets of silver were made
To give warning of an enemy raid,
Or during good weather
To bring people together
And maybe to start a parade.

Numbers 13: 1-2: And the Lord spake unto Moses, saying, Send thou men, that they may search the land of Canaan, which I give unto the children of Israel: of every tribe of their fathers shall ye send a man, every one a ruler among them.

It shouldn't come as a surprise
That Moses enlisted some spies,
One from each tribe,
And maybe a scribe,
To investigate Canaan and advise.

Numbers 13: 25: And they returned from searching of the land after forty days.

Here's something worthy of praise
The spies searched Canaan 40 days>
It could have been seven
Or even eleven
But the default number is 40; always.

Numbers 13: 33: And there we saw the giants, the sons of Anak, which come of the giants: and we were in our own sight as grasshoppers, and so we were in their sight.

Yes, there were giants in those days
With stature that today would amaze.
But we have a few

That are seven foot two
And are busy learning basketball plays.

Numbers 14: 18: The Lord is long suffering, and of great mercy, forgiving iniquity and transgression, and by no means clearing the guilty, visiting the iniquity of the fathers upon the children unto the third and fourth generation.

Do you remember Noah and Canaan,
Back before the Jews were a clan?
It isn't too odd,
According to God,
To pay for the sins of the old man.

Numbers 15: 8,10 : And when thou preparest a bullock for a burnt offering, or for a sacrifice in performing a vow, or peace offerings unto the Lord: And thou shalt bring for a drink offering half an hin of wine . . .

When offering a young male bovine
Bring also a half hin of good wine.
If you have found
Somewhere around
A field full of fruit of the vine.

Number 15: 26: And it shall be forgiven all the congregation of the children of Israel, and the stranger that sojourneth among them; seeing all the people were in ignorance.

If it's the Israelite's contention
That they never heard Moses mention,
Any laws or decrees
And knew not of these
They would not suffer God's intervention.

Numbers 16: 30: But if the Lord make a new thing, and the earth open her mouth, and swallow them up, with all that appertain unto them, and they go down quick into the pit; then ye shall understand that these men have provoked the Lord.
And the earth opened her mouth, and swallowed them up, and their houses, and all the men that appertained unto Korah, and all their goods.

> Don't complain or provoke the Lord
> And don't even foment discord,
> Or a sink-hole may
> Appear one nice day
> And swallow you and your horde.

Numbers 16: 32: And the earth opened her mouth, and swallowed them up, and their houses, and all the men that appertained unto Korah, and all their goods.

> Sometimes God's angels did the killing
> Whether or not they were willing.
> The plague killed some others,
> Whether children or mothers,
> And falling in a sink-hole was chilling.

Numbers 17: 5, 8: And it shall come to pass, that the man's rod, whom I shall choose, shall blossom;
And it came to pass, that on the morrow Moses went into the tabernacle of witness; and behold, the rod of Aaron for the house of Levi was budded and brought forth buds, and bloomed blossoms, and yielded almonds.

> A secret of those in the know
> That a finding next morning would show
> Of those in the room
> The rod that would bloom
> Would be Aaron's, Moses' bro.

Numbers 35: 11, 13: Then ye shall appoint you cities to be cities of refuge for you; that the slayer may flee thither, which killeth any person unawares. . . And of these cities which ye shall give six cities shall ye have for refuge.

> Are sanctuary cities something new?
> I think I can name quite a few.
> But it was God's plan
> To make refuge for a man
> If someone, somehow, he slew.

Numbers 36: 11: For Mablah, Tirzah, and Hoglah, and Milcah, and Noah, the daughters of Zelophehad, were married into their father's brother's sons;

> To protect the tribal inheritance
> It's best to marry an acquaintance.
> The marriage of cousins
> Of which there were dozens
> Occurred more often than with aunts.

Like Leviticus, Numbers features the Lord, Moses and Aaron with about a million supporting actors. It gives us a fairly complete account of how the Israelites existed in what is called the wilderness of the Sinai (and Etham, and Sin, and Paran, and Zin) for 40 years. We know what they ate, where they camped, how they dressed and who the Lord chose to perform the tasks required for living in the deserts or oases they encountered.

The last chapters of Numbers are devoted to the division of the territory Canaan among the twelve tribes, taking special care, since Moses was a Levite, to insure that the Levites, or priests, would be taken care of. Only when you are sure that God has your back can you make plans to divide the territory even before you have occupied it.

CHAPTER 5

DEUTERONOMY

According to a 1943 theory, the book of Deuteronomy was added later than the other books of Moses. It was composed somewhat differently than the other four books, known as the Tetrateuch, and has been classified with Joshua and through the books of Kings as the 'Deuteronomistic history'. Be that as it may, the Torah continues to contain 5 books, known by Christians as the 'five books of Moses', or the Pentateuch.

Many have claimed that this book cannot have been written by Moses because it describes his death and burial. This may be true but it is only in the last chapter of the book that his demise is recorded. Another Levite may have added this obituary to conclude the life of Moses. While other books of the Torah seem to have been written by other hands than that of Moses, we can justly believe that Moses may have authored some of the text that it is assumed he had written but other words were penned by different scribes.

In any case, Deuteronomy explains the rules and directions for the possession of the lands promised by God to Abraham, Isaac, and Jacob, and which includes Israel today.

Deuteronomy 1: 3-4: And it came to pass in the fortieth year....that
Moses spake unto the children of Israel...
After he had slain Sihon the king of the Amorites, which dwelt in
Heshbon, and Og the king of Bashan, which dwelt in Astaroth in Edrei:

> The Lord was not the only one killing,
> Moses himself thought it was thrilling.
> King Sihon he slew
> And King Og, too.
> The way that he killed them was chilling.

Deuteronomy 2: 32-33: Then Sihon came out against us, he and all his
people, to fight at Jahaz.
And the Lord our God delivered him before us; and we smote him, and
his sons, and all his people.

> The Bible at times can be boring
> Even those verses about warring.
> The Israelites slew
> More than a few.
> Do you find most genocide deploring?

Deuteronomy 4: 25, 27: When thou.....shall corrupt yourselves, and....
do evil in the sight of the Lord thy God, to provoke him to anger.
And the Lord shall scatter you among the nations, and ye shall be left
few in number among the heathen, whether the Lord shall lead you.

> Hundreds of years ago, Moses foresaw
> That the people might ignore God's law.
> So he issued a warning
> That one future morning
> They again might make bricks without straw.

Deuteronomy 4:40: Thou shalt keep therefore his statutes, and his commandments, which I command thee this day, that it may go well with thee, and with thy children after thee, and that thou mayest prolong thy days upon the earth, which the Lord thy God giveth thee, for ever.

> Some prophets make only guesses
> But Moses in one of his addresses,
> Foretold of the wages
> They'd reap thru the ages
> If they didn't control their excesses.

Deuteronomy 5: 7: Thou shalt have none other gods before me.

> Worshipping many gods can be fun;
> Gods of rivers, of seas, and the sun.
> Pray to the light
> Or worship at night
> But consider Lord God Number One.

Deuteronomy 5: 8: Thou shalt not make thee any graven image, or any likeness of any thing that is in heaven above, or that is in the earth beneath, or that is in the waters beneath the earth.

> A likeness can mean any thing.
> Graven tho refers to carving.
> Thus the Lord outlawed
> Praying to another god
> For only praising Him shall ye sing.

Deuteronomy 5: 11: Thou shalt not take the name of the Lord thy God in vain.

> Use god's name, but not in vain.
> Use it when praying for rain,

Or when the Lord you praise,
Or in Christmas plays,
Or when you experience great pain.

Deuteronomy 5: 12: Keep the sabbath day to sanctify it…..

Back in Genesis Two, God rested.
He sanctified a day and he blest it.
It's Shabbat to Jews
But in other folks views
Different names have been suggested.

Deuteronomy 5: 16: Honor thy father and thy mother…..

You may not care for your mother,
And can't stand her significant other.
But one thing is true
They forgave you
When you were mean to your brother.

Deuteronomy 5: 17: Thou shalt not kill.

The Lord issued a sixth caveat,
Which may be ignored in combat.
It may be your skill,
But thou shalt not kill.
Trust your Lord God to do that.

Deuteronomy 5: 18: Neither shalt thou commit adultery.

Not many would think it was nice
To practice a particular vice.
The sacrament of marriage

You should not disparage.
One partner in life should suffice.

Deuteronomy 5: 19: Neither shalt thou steal.

It says, Thou shalt not steal.
Valjean stole bread for a meal.
What would you do
For a little beef stew?
When it's the pangs of hunger you feel.

Deuteronom 5: 20: Neither shalt thou bear false witness against thy neighbor.

False witness we know is to lie.
To lie is to falsely testify.
Even out of court
Do not report
That aliens took you up in the sky.

Deuteronomy 5: 21: Neither shalt thou desire thy neighbour's wife, neither shalt thou covet thy neighbour's house, his field, or his manservant, or his maidservant, his ox, or his ass, or any thing that is thy neighbor's.

Coveting is just a brief thought.
It doesn't really matter a lot.
The house cross the street
Most surely is neat
You wish it was one you had bought.

Deuteronomy 7: 15: And the Lord will take away from thee all sickness, and will put none of the evil diseases of Egypt, which thou knows, upon thee; but will lay them upon all them that hate thee.

Have you better insurance with Triple A?
Or Mercury, Hartford, or USAA?
When you can afford
To trust in the Lord
And keep all Egypt's sickness away.

Deuteronomy 9: 11: And it came to pass at the end of forty days and forty nights, that the Lord gave me the two tables of stone, even the tables of the covenant.

To get two tables from Yahweh
Moses was required to stay
Forty days and nights
Up on the heights.
He was happy to finally get away.

Deuteronomy 9: 17: And I took the two tables, and cast them out of my hands, and brake them before your eyes.

From Mt Sinai Moses finally descended.
The visit with his God had now ended.
He cast to the ground
The tablets he'd found
They shattered and could not be mended.

Deuteronomy 10: 1-2: At that time the Lord said unto me, Hew thee two tables of stone like unto the first, and come up unto me into the mount and make thee an ark of wood.
And I will write on the tables the words that were in the first tables which thou breakest, and thou shalt put them in the ark.

So Moses went back up the hill
Something like old Jack and Jill.
And there he stayed

While the Lord God remade
The decrees such as "Thou shall not kill".

*Deuteronomy 11: 30 : Are they not on the other side of Jordan, by the
way where the sun goeth down, in the land of the Canaanites, which
dwell in the champaign over against Gilgal, beside the plains of Moreh?*

Geography the Lord knew quite well.
It's very clear He was able to tell
Which valley or plain
The people would maintain
In the land where they shortly would dwell.

*Deuteronomy 20: 16-17: But of the cities of these people, which the Lord
thy God give thee for an inheritance, thou shalt save alive nothing that
breatheth:....But thou shalt utterly destroy them; namely, the Hittites,
and the Amorites, the Canaanites, and the Perizzites, the Hivites, and
the Jebusites; as the Lord thy God hath commanded thee:*

The Bible says the Israelites slew
A thousand?, a million or two.
But how many died
On the Israelite side?
History reflects the winning side's view.

*Deuteronomy 34: 4-5: And the Lord said unto him, This is the land
which I sware unto Abraham, unto Isaac, and unto Jacob, saying, I will
give it unto thy seed: I have caused thee to see it with thine eyes, but thou
shalt not go over thither.*
*So Moses the servant of the Lord died there in the land of Moab,
according to the word of the Lord.*

After Moses had relayed God's word,
And he knew that the people had heard,

In Moab he died
And the people, they cried
But their future in Canaan was secured.

Deuteronomy 34: 10: And there arose not a prophet since in Israel like unto Moses, whom the Lord knew face to face.

As expected, when Moses died
With Joshua there by his side,
For at least several days
He was routinely praised
And occasionally almost deified.

Although the book of Joshua claims great victories by the Israelites including the cities they destroyed and people they slew, most biblical scholars today believe that the Israelites gradually migrated to Canaan (or were indigenous) and lived, as shepherds, on the peripheries of the cities. Recent archaeological discoveries point to this conclusion. Historical documents indicate that the Israelites occupied territories known as Israel and Judah in the levant with Phoenicians and other small groups claiming territory along the Mediterranean coast.

CHAPTER 6

JOSHUA

With Joshua we have the beginnings of Books of the Bible named after individuals. Although Moses didn't have his book, the Levites, of which he was a leader, had their own book. Joshua, chosen by Moses to succeed him, turned out to be a good leader, and with God's help was able to carry out God's plan of conquest and settlement in spite of the fact that little, if any, evidence of his activities or victories have been uncovered by the archaeologists who have searched, lo these many decades. Many modern scholars believe that the Israelites may have been indigenous inhabitants of Canaan or may have entered over hundreds of years and grazed their herds at the periphery of Canaanite cities and villages.

Be that as it may, the stories which make up the book of Joshua, from the spies' encounter with the woman Rahab to the death, at one hundred and ten years, of Joshua, seem to be great enough to give the present inhabitants of Israel justification for their possession of the ancient land of Canaan.

Joshua 2: 1, 6: And Joshua the son of Nun sent out of Shittim two men to spy secretly, saying, Go view the land, even Jericho. And they went, and came into an harlot's house, named Rahab, and lodged there.

But she had brought them up to the roof of the house, and hid them with the stalks of flax......

> In Jericho the spies met a maid
> Who provided them with much needed aid.
> So they could relax
> She hid them in flax
> In case of a Canaanite raid.

Joshua 3: 10: And Joshua said, Hereby ye shall know that the living God is among you, and that he will without fail drive out from before you the Canaanites, and the Hittites, and the Hivites, and the Perizzites, and the Girgashites, and the Amorites, and the Jebusites.

> God drove out the Amorites,
> The Canaanites and Jebusites,
> And maybe those
> That God chose
> And were not known to be Semites.

Joshua 3: 17: And the priests that bare the ark of the covenant of the Lord stood firm on dry ground in the midst of Jordan, and all the Israelites passed over on dry ground, until all the people were passed clean over Jordan.

> No matter if a river is wide
> One way to get to the other side
> If you can't fly
> But want to keep dry
> Use the Ark of Covenant as your guide.

Joshua 6: 4: And seven priests shall bear before the ark seven trumpets of rams' horns: and the seventh day ye shall compass the city seven times, and the priests shall blow with the trumpets.

Once again there's the number seven,
One of three sacred to Heaven.
Around old Jericho
Seven times they go
It could very well have been eleven.

Joshua 6: 16, 20, 22: And it came to pass at the seventh time, when the priests blew with the trumpets, Joshua said unto the people, Shout; for the Lord hath given you the city. . . and the people shouted with a great shout, that the wall fell down flat,. . . but Joshua had said unto the two men...go into the harlot's house, and bring out thence the woman....

At the signal the people began to shout
And before the Swordsmen roamed about
Jericho's wall
Began to fall
Two men led Rahab's family out.

Joshua 6: 20: . . . and the people shouted with a great shout, that the wall fell down flat, so that the people went up into the city, every man straight before him, and they took the city.

Jericho is an old, old town.
The walls were easy to blow down.
It took about
One real loud shout
To make the town so renown.

Joshua 6: 19: But all the silver, and gold, and vessels brass and iron, are consecrated to the Lord; and they shall come into the treasury of the Lord.

The Levites, or God, had decided
Gold and silver would not be divided.
It belongs to the Lord

As his just reward
For all the help He provided.

Joshua 7: 24, 25: And Joshua, and all Israel with him, took Achan the son of Zerah. . . and all that he had . . . to the valley of Achor.
And Joshua said, Why hast thou troubled us? the Lord shall trouble thee this day. And all Israel stoned him with stones, and burned them with fire,

Old Achan's sins weren't atoned,
Cause they took everything that he owned.
And set the entire
Collection on fire
They say the whole family was stoned.

Joshua 10: 3, 4, 10: Wherefore Adonizedec king of Jerusalem sent unto (the kings of Hebron, Jarmuth, Latish, and Eglon).
Come up unto me, and help me, that we may smite Gibeon:
And the Lord discomfited them before Israel, and slew them with a great slaughter at Gibeon . . . .

It doesn't take the Lord long to decide
When it's best to commit homicide.
So if it's war,
Which we may abhor,
Let's hope the Lord's on our side.

Joshua 10: 11: And it came to pass, as they fled before Israel, and were in the going down to Bethhoron, that the Lord cast down great stones from heaven upon them unto Azekah, and they died; they were more which died with hailstones than they whom the children of Israel slew with the sword

The Lord stored up in his heaven
A multitude of ways to kill men.
One not likely to fail

Was golf ball sized hail
Tho golf balls weren't known way back then.

*Joshua 11: 10, 11: And Joshua at that time turned back, and took
Hazor, and smote the king thereof with the sword. . .
And they smote all the souls that were therein with the edge of the sword
utterly destroying them:*

> Joshua, in the biblical record,
> Smote armies with the edge of the sword.
> They used daggers to stab
> And occasionally jab.
> What weapon was used by the Lord?

*Joshua 21: 3, 41: And the children of Israel gave unto the Levites out
of their inheritance, at the command of the Lord, these cities and their
suburbs. . . . All the cities of the Levites within the possession of the
children of Israel were forty and eight cities with their suburbs.*

> When all the killing had ceased
> A few hundred thousand, at least,
> The land was divided
> And God then decided
> Every tribe have some land and a priest.

The book of Joshua ultimately lists the kings of the cities of Canaan
that were slaughtered by Joshua, his army or God. These numbered
31 kings from cities that frequently can be found in atlases of the
Bible. The atlases may also indicate the geographical territories
that were assigned to the various tribes of Israelites as detailed in
Joshua. These conquests were followed by a period of peace before
the invasions of Hittites, Egyptians, Assyrians, and Babylonians.
Subsequently we will find Greeks and Romans encroaching on
Israelite territory.

CHAPTER 7

JUDGES

Although the Israelites had no king during their first few decades in Canaan there evidently were judges who led the various tribes in collective endeavors such as wars and smitings. The book of Judges refers to several of these judges and some of their adventures.

The campaign against the tribe of Benjamin is unique in that the casualties suffered by Israelites are mentioned, whereas in previous accounts the Israelites might smite ten thousand enemy but no mention is made of the number of Israelites left on the battlefield.

This is also the book that relates the birth, youth and ultimate death of the famous strong man, Samson, who seems to enjoy deceiving his wife Delilah.

Samson, however, strong but dumb like Lenny in Steinbeck's "Of Mice and Men", seems not to have understood what Delilah's plans were and finally informed her that his strength was in his curly locks.

Others who earned a mention in the book of Judges include Barak, Gideon, Abimelech and Jephthah. When the Israelites did evil in the sight of the Lord He sold or delivered them into the hands of their enemies. Subsequently, God chose a judge to liberate the subjugated Israelites.

Judges 1: 1-2: Now after the death of Joshua it came to pass, that the children of Israel asked the Lord, saying, Who shall go up for us against the Canaanites first, to fight against them?
And the Lord said, Judah shall go up: behold, I have delivered the land into his hand.

> The Lord didn't seem to care
> How many died in warfare.
> When He delivered the land
> Into Judah's own hand
> The odds seemed a little unfair.

Judges 1: 12-13: And Caleb said, He that smiteth Kirjathsepher, and taketh it, to him will I give Achsah my daughter to wife.
And Othniel the son of Lenaz, Caleb's younger brother, took it; and he gave him Achsah his daughter to wife.

> Talk about your spoils of war
> I don't know if you knew this before
> But you can win a wife
> If you risk your life
> And kill ten thousand enemy, or more.

Judges 1: 15: And she said unto him, Give me a blessing: for thou has given me a south land; give me also springs of water. And Caleb gave her the upper springs and the nether springs.

> Though she had land near the shore
> Caleb's daughter wanted even more.
> Like some hot springs

And a few other things.
Hotels there now? more than four.

Judges 3: 29: And they slew of Moab at that time about ten thousand men, all lusty, and all men of valour; and there escaped not a man.

Why do we still read of fighting?
Aren't we all weary of smiting?
I'll offer some advice
The Psalms they are nice
But wars are much more exciting.

Judges 4: 1,2: And the children of Israel again did evil in the sight of the Lord, when Ehud was dead.
And the Lord sold them into the hand of Jabin king of Canaan, that reigned in Hazor; the captain of whose host was Sisera, which dwelt in Harosheth of the Gentiles.

Because of the evil that they did
The Lord God again became livid.
The Israelites were sold
For a few ephahs of gold.
How could they have been so stupid?

Numbers 31: 7: Judges. 6: 1: And they warred against the Midianites, as the Lord commanded Moses; and they slew all the males.......And the children of Israel did evil in the sight of the Lord; and the Lord delivered them into the hand of Midian seven years,

The Lord knew the evil that was done
But he forgot about Numbers 31.
It was way back then
Moses killed all the men,
Every Midianite father and son

Judges 6: 25: And it came to pass the same night, that the Lord said unto him, Take thy father's young bullock, even the second bullock of seven years old, and throw down the alter of Baal that thy father hath, and cut down the grove that is by it.

Baal was a storm god, you see
Dating back to 2348 BCE.
As was Marduk and Enlil
And Zeus on his hill,
And the Chinese dragon, certainly.

Judges 7: 2: And the Lord said unto Gideon, The people that are with thee are too many for me to give the Midianites into their hands, lest Israel vaunt themselves against me, saying, Mine own hand hath saved me.

The Lord chose Gideon to lead
And he reluctantly agreed.
But God said then
You've too many men.
So he only took those he would need.

Judges 8: 33, 10: 5,6 : And it came to pass, as soon as Gideon was dead, that the children of Israel turned again, and went a whoring after Ba'al-im, and made Ba'al-be'rith their god.
And Ja'ir died, and was buried in Camon. And the children of Israel did evil again in the sight of the Lord, and served Ba'al-im, and Ash'ta-roth and the gods of Syria....

The judges who died were missed.
Gideon and Jair are on the list.
When they passed
The people at last
Worshipped any god that they wished.

Judges 16: 6: And Delilah said to Samson, Tell me, I pray thee, wherein thy great strength lieth, and wherewith thou mightest be bound to afflict thee.

> You know "Samson and Delilah" I'm sure
> The movie starring Victor Mature?
> The other star?
> Hedy Lamarr.
> A story adapted from scripture.

Supposedly, the book of Judges relates the events that befell the Israelites once they insinuated themselves into the Canaanite culture. It makes sure we understand that the Israelites did not destroy every city and hamlet that they encountered. They lived among the natives and, because of their occasional worshipping of foreign gods, angered the Lord and, at His behest, were frequently subjugated by neighboring tribes such as the Midianites and the Philistines.

God, however, was always willing to provide a 'savior' who, with the Lord's help, was able to free the Israelites from their servitude as he did in Egypt. Thus we hear of Othniel the son of Kenaz, Ehud the son of Gera, Shamgar son of Anath, Barak the son of Abinoam, and Gideon. Well, we have at least heard of Gideon the son of Joash, if only because of the Bibles that you may find in the endtable drawer in your hotel room.

Many biographies of Benjamin tend to skip the part of Judges wherein the other tribes of Israel war against the Benjaminites who lost around eighty-three thousand men because certain men in a Benjaminite town had caused the death of one woman. Talk about sibling rivalry.

After peace was declared there was a problem. The remaining men of the tribe of Benjamin could not find wives. We must assume that many women were killed in the fires set by the children of Israel or who had been slain by the edge of the sword. Fortunately, there were a few women and virgins who were betrothed to the few men of Benjamin

CHAPTER 8

RUTH, SAMUEL I & II

The reasons the short book of Ruth is included in the Holy Book is because 1) she was a descendant of Lot, and 2) she was the ancestor of King David. We can therefore contend that she was an Adamite, being of the line of Adam and Noah. Boaz, her husband, was a resident of Bethlehem and therefore probably also an Adamite.

Ruth did what a multitude of women have done since; she married the boss. Maybe that is why she joined the select group of men whose stories are included in the Bible, but I will stick with the reasons in 1) and 2) above.

The books of Samuel finally introduce us to the Israelite kingship with the divine coronation of Saul. The new king displeases Samuel and the Lord by not following God's exact plans. In other words, he did evil in the sight of the Lord by not killing all the livestock that had been condemned.

This leads to the introduction of David, son of Jesse, onto the scene, with his employment as a shepherd, a player of the harp and an expert with a sling. We all know the conclusion of the story of 'David and Goliath' where David, with his Lord's help, slew the 9 foot giant, winning the day.

Instead of ruling like a king should, Saul spent much of his and his soldiers' time unsuccessfully pursuing young David.

Ruth 1: 3-5: And Elimelech, Naomi's husband, died; and she was left, and her two sons Mahlon and Chilion. And they took them wives of the women of Moab; the name of the one was Orpah, and the name of the other Ruth: and they dwelled there about ten years. And Mahlon and Chilion died also both of them…..

> A princess Ruth of Moab was not.
> As a widow, a new husband she sought.
> Her claim to fame
> Was not her name
> Nor as a great great granddaughter of Lot.

Ruth 4: 13, 16-17: So Boaz took Ruth, and she was his wife; and when he went in unto her, the Lord gave her conception, and she bare a son…….and they called his name Obed: he is the father of Jesse, the father of David.

> David was a great Israelite king
> The youngest of father Jesse's offspring.
> His great grandmother
> Was no one other
> Than Ruth, famous for just that one thing.

I Samuel 1: 13-15: Now Hannah, she spoke in her heart; only her lips moved, but her voice was not heard: therefore Eli thought she had been drunken… And Eli said unto her, How long wilt thou be drunken? put away thy wine from thee….And Hannah answered and said, No, my lord, I am a woman of sorrowful spirit: I have drunk neither wine nor strong drink, but have poured out my soul before the Lord.

There's Hannah. No one was sweeter.
She had a sister who would maltreat her.
Even those near her
Could not even hear her.
Luckily priest Eli was a lip-reader.

I Samuel 3: 20: And all Israel from Dan to Beersheba knew that Samuel was established to be a prophet of the Lord.

Well, Samuel had no PhD
But was good at prophesy.
By going in a trance
God's words he'd enhance
And predict events that would be.

I Samuel 4: 10, 13: And the Philistines fought, and Israel was smitten, and they fled every man into his tent: and there was a very great slaughter; for there fell of Israel thirty thousand footmen,

A multitude of city people cried
When told 30,000 soldiers had died
Attempting to halt
A Philistine assault.
But at least we know they had tried.

I Samuel 5: 11,12: So they sent and gathered together all the lords of the Philistines, and said, Send away the ark of the God of Israel, and let it go again to his own place, that it slay us not, and our people: for there was a deadly destruction throughout all the city; the hand of God was very heavy there. And the men that died not were smitten with the tumors: and the cry of the city went up to heaven.

Keeping the ark can cause tumors
If not many disgusting humors.

So heed what they say
And send the ark away.
But maybe they are unfounded rumors.

I Samuel 11: 15 / 14: 47 / 15: 9: And all the people went to Gilgal; there they made Saul king before the Lord in Gilgal. . . . So Saul took the kingdom over Israel, and fought against all his enemies on every side.... But Saul and the people spared Agag. . .

The Israelites finally had a king
Which was a mixed blessing.
Between Saul and his son
Many battles were won,
But sparing the enemy's an evil thing.

I Samuel 16: 11, 13: And Samuel said unto Jesse, Are here all thy children? And he said, There remaineth yet the youngest, and, behold, he keepeth the sheep. . . Then Samuel took the horn of oil, and anointed him in the midst of his brethren: and the Spirit of the Lord came upon David. .

David was Jesse's youngest son.
Samuel said he was the one
To be anointed with oil
This boy of the soil.
His journey to fame had begun.

I Samuel 17: 34,35: And David said unto Saul, Thy servant kept his father's sheep, and there came a lion, and a bear, and took a lamb out of the flock: And I went out after him, and smote him, and delivered it out of his mouth:

David said there was a lion and bear
Roaming wild somewhere out there.

It does not say
In exactly what way
He ended up slaughtering the pair.

I Samuel 17: 4,5: And there went out a champion out of the camp of the Philistines, named Goliath, of Gath, whose height was six cubits and a span. . . And he had an helmet of brass upon his head, and he was armed with a coat of mail; and the weight of the coat was five thousand shekels of brass.

Goliath was pumped up with pride.
With armor he was well supplied.
But David had a feel'in
That he surely would win
The good Lord was there at his side.

*1 Samuel 16: 21 / 17: 55: And David came to Saul, and stood before him: and he loved him greatly; and he became his armourbearer.
And when Saul saw David go forth against the Philistine, he said unto Abner, the captain of the host, Abner, whose son is this youth? And Abner said, As thy soul liveth, O king, I cannot tell.*

Though David worked for King Saul
It was no time at all
The king forgot
And knew him not
What other things didn't he recall?

I Samuel 18: 25: And Saul said, Thus shall ye say to David, The king desireth not any dowry, but an hundred forskins of the Philistines, to be avenged of the king's enemies. But Saul thought to make David fall by the hand of the Philistines.

David was from the Benjamins.
His record shows many wins.
To earn him a wife
To share his life
He brought in two hundred four skins.

I Samuel 19:20: And Saul sent messengers to take David: and when they saw the company of the prophets prophesying, and Samuel standing as appointed over them, the Spirit of God was upon the messengers of Saul, and they also prophesied.

If a prophet you wish to be
So the future you could foresee,
Wait for the Spirit
No need to fear it
For God will bring it to thee.

1 Samuel 23: 15: 24: 6: And David saw that Saul was come out to seek his life: and David was in the wilderness of Ziph in a wood. . . And he said unto his men, The Lord forbid that I should do this thing unto my master, the Lord's anointed, to stretch forth mine hand against him, seeing he is the anointed of the Lord.

David had smitten a Philistine
When he was just a mere teen,
But against a king
He did not a thing
King Saul is the one that we mean.

I Samuel. 25: 42-43 And Abigail hasted, and arose, and rode upon an ass, with five damsels of hers that went after her; and she went after the messengers of David, and became his wife. David also took Ahinoam of Jezebel; and they were both of them his wives.

As for women, a man should have a few.
It's a poor man who has only two.
One who cooks,
One for looks,
And sixteen more if you're Hebrew.

I Samuel 29: 9: And Achish answered and said unto David, I know that thou art good in my sight, as an angel of God: notwithstanding the princes of the Philistines have said, He shall not go up with us to the battle.

The Philistines and David agreed.
His safety was now guaranteed.
But he wouldn't fight
It wouldn't be right
Let someone else do the terrible deed.

The first book of Samuel covers his birth and his successes as he smites the Philistines and meets Saul. They both are prophets for it is easy to qualify as a prophet (I Samuel. 19: 20-21). Since almost anyone can stop and prophesy, it might be more accurate to assume that they meditated rather than forecasting future events. The most helpful, however, were those who, like in a seance, could 'bring up' the dead (I Samuel. 28: 11-15) for whatever reason.

One Samuel takes us from Joseph to Saul and to David. It is apparent that Saul wants his son Jonathan to succeed him as king of the Israelites and therefore he (Saul) is determined to get rid of the competition, David, although he predicts that David shall become king of Israel (I Samuel 24: 20).

With the help of Saul's son Jonathan, and others, David is able to elude the pursuing armies of Saul and even retires to the lands of his enemies, Moab and Philistine, where he and his 400 man army continue to smite enemies left and right.

Saul even offers David his daughter, Merab, who is finally given to Adriel, the Meholathite, and then his daughter Michal whom David married. When king Saul gave Michal, David's wife, to Phalti, the son of Laish, David married Abigail the widow of Nabal, who had been smitten by the Lord, and Ahinoam of Jezebel.

Ultimately, Saul and his sons were killed in battle with the Philistines who had denied David the chance to smite the king Saul. In the following book, II Samuel, more adventures of the future king of Israel will be encountered.

2 Samuel 1: 11-12: Then David took hold of his clothes, and rent them; and likewise all the men who were with him: And they mourned, and wept, and fasted until even, for Saul, and for Jonathan his son, and for the people of the Lord, and for the house of Israel; because they were fallen by the sword.

> David was quite frequently resented,
> And all David's men seemed demented.
> They mourned and wept,
> Even a fast they kept
> And the clothes they wore were all rented.

2 Samuel 2: 18 / 4: 5: And there were three sons of Zeruiah there, Joab, and Abishai, and Asahel: and Asahel was as light of foot as a wild roe. And the sons of Rimmon the Beerothite, Rehab and Baanah, went, and came about the heat of the day to the house of Ishbosheth, who lay on a bed at noon.

> I think it's time to announce,
> Biblical names you can pronounce

Are the ones you remember
From May to December,
But David's the one name that counts.

2 Samuel 5: 12,13 : And David perceived that the Lord had established him king over Israel, and that he had exalted his kingdom for his people Israel's sake.
And David took him more concubines and wives out of Jerusalem, after he was come from Hebron: and there were yet sons and daughters born to David.

Who is the star of Samuel Two?
It's the Torah's most notable Hebrew
He possessed such fame
We remember his name
David, one memorable Jew.

2 Samuel 8: 11,12: Which also king David did dedicate unto the Lord, with the silver and gold that he had dedicated of all nations which he had subdued; of Syria, and of Moab, and of the children of Ammon, and of the Philistines, and of Amalek, and of the spoil of Hadadezer, son of Rehab, king of Zobah.

David, with thirty thousand men
Slew whole armies; six or seven,
And he slew them with sword
With help from his Lord
In ten years he may do it again.

2 Samuel 9: 3, 6: And the king said, Is there yet not any of the house of Saul, that I may show the kindness of God unto him? And Ziba said unto the king, Jonathan hath yet a son, which is lame on his feet.
Now when Mephibosheth, the son of Jonathan, son of Saul, was come unto David, he fell on his face, and did reverence.

Mephibosheth was a grandson of Saul.
He was lame, as you will recall.
He met the king
Late in the spring
And did reverence to him in the fall.

2 Samuel 11: 4, 14,15: And David sent messengers and took her; and she came in unto him, and he lay with her; for she was purified from her cleanliness: and she returned unto her house.
And it came to pass in the morning, that David wrote a letter to Joab, and sent it by the hand of Uriah. And he wrote in the letter, saying, Set ye Uriah in the forefront of the hottest battle, and retire ye from him, that he may be smitten, and die.

Now David was a very prudent man
Avoiding trouble whenever he can.
When a wife caught his eye
The husband must die
A job he left to his henchman.

2 Samuel 12: 9,10: Wherefore hast thou despised the commandment of the Lord, to do evil in his sight? thou hast killed Uriah the Hittite with the sword, and hast taken his wife to be thy wife, and hast slain him with the sword of the children of Ammon.

David smote a number of Ammonites
And even some valiant Moabites.
Then one Hittite
David did smite.
This killing, God's anger incites.

2 Samue. 18: 14: Then said Joab, I may not tarry thus with thee. And he took three darts in his hand, and thrust them through the heart of Absalom, while he was yet alive in the midst of the oak.

Absolom, who got hung up on an oak,
Died when Joab gave him a poke
With a dart
To the heart
They thought he had died of a stroke.

David was unfortunate to have King Saul follow him around with the intent to kill. But fortunately God was on David's side and David pleaded and bargained with Saul but to no avail. Saul desired to have his son Jonathan succeed him on the throne and David was a threat to that dream.

More devastating, however, must have been the unfaithfulness of his son Absalom who began to collect followers and allies among the people of Israel and set himself up as chief in Hebron. Instead of confronting or joining battle with his son, David, as with Saul, avoided contact and took steps to evade the spies and warriors of Absalom.

Finally, when Absalom was killed by Joab and his men, the people, including David, mourned. It was an outcome that David had tried to prevent.

CHAPTER 9

KINGS AND CHRONICLES

The books of Kings, I and II, continue the adventures of the great kings of Israel/Judah. Saul is dead, David is elderly, and the son of David and Bathsheba, Solomon, mentioned once in II Samuel, is the leading contender among those who want to succeed their father David.

David has the presence of mind to elevate his son Solomon to the kingship and, Solomon, drunk with power, tells his hitman, Benaiah, to eliminate possible trouble-makers such as Adonijah, Joab, and Shimei. King Solomon shows his appreciation of Benaiah's work by granting him Joab's job as head of the military.

And, of no consequence, we find the queen of Sheba (a community either in Yemen or across the Red Sea in Ethiopia) coming to Jerusalem with a large contingent of camels and servants, praising Solomon and exchanging gifts. Then she departed to the mysterious land of Sheba.

The division of Hebrew Canaan into two parts is related in this book. Jeroboam is king of Israel and Rehoboam rules over the tribes of Judah and Benjamin in Judah. The histories of Assyria, Babylonia and Persia mention the conquering of Israel and Judea.

In the Chronicles Hebrew women are mentioned because they gave birth to prominent (at least noteworthy) men. Boaz is indicated as the father of Jesse, the father of David. Ruth, David's great grandmother, gets no credit.

Supposedly, the chronicle records are from temple collections which may have been available to the authors of the books.

1 Kings 1: 1-2: Now king David was old and stricken in years; and they covered him with clothes, but he gat no heat.
Wherefore his servants said unto him, let there be sought for my lord the king a young virgin: and let her stand before the king, and let her cherish him, and let her lie in thy bosom, that my lord may get heat.

> It seems young virgins are hot,
> Though some would say they are not.
> Bathsheba was old
> And probably cold,
> So a virgin for David was sought.

1 Kings 5: 13-15: And King Solomon conscripted forced labor out of all Israel; and the levy was thirty thousand men.
And he sent them to Lebanon, ten thousand a month by courses: a month they were in Lebanon, and two months at home.
And Solomon had three score and ten thousand that bored burdens, and four score hewers in the mountains.

> Men sent to Lebanon: thirty thousand.
> Eighty thousand were hewers in woodland.
> One month they would hew
> Then go home for two
> A schedule they thought was just grand.

1 Kings 10: 1,2: And when the queen of Sheba heard of the fame of Solomon concerning the name of the Lord, she came to prove him with hard questions. And she came to Jerusalem with a very great train, with camels that bare spices, and very much gold, and precious stones: and when she was come to Solomon, she communed with him of all that was in her heart.

> Solomon had a queen as a visitor.
> She brought spices, gold and much more.
> She limited her stays
> To a couple of days
> She was Sheba's sole ambassador.

1 Kings 11: : And he had seven hundred wives, princesses, and three hundred concubines; and his wives turned away his heart.

> Solomon knew every wife's name.
> For twenty of them t'was the same.
> And in many foreign tongue
> Songs to strange gods were sung.
> That he ignored the princess was a shame.

1 Kings 11: 19: And Hadad found great favor in the sight of Pharaoh, so that he gave him to wife the sister of his own wife, the sister of Tahpenes the queen.

> The authors call Egypt's kings, Pharaoh.
> Most of their names they didn't know.
> And queen Tahpenes
> Was she wife of king Menes?
> No, she was wed to pharaoh so and so.

1 Kings 11: 30-3: And Ahijah caught the new garment that was on him, and rent it in twelve pieces:

And he said to Jeroboam, Take thee ten pieces: for thus saith the Lord, the God of Israel, Behold, I will rend the kingdom out of the hand of Solomon, and will give ten tribes to thee:

> According to the Biblical scribes
> The book of 1 Kings describes
> The reign of Jeroboam
> And that of Rehoboam
> Who ended up with only two tribes.

1 Kings 15: 5, 2 Samuel. 12: 9: Because David did that which was right in the eyes of the Lord, and turned not aside from any thing that he commanded him all the days of his life, save only in the matter of Uriah the Hittite.....Wherefore hast thou despised the commandment of the Lord, to do evil in his sight? thou hast killed Uriah the Hittite with the sword, and hast taken his wife to be thy wife, and hast slain him with the sword the children of Ammon.

> Now David was perfect in God's sight,
> Except the matter with Uriah the Hittite.
> So what's a mere life
> When you inherit the wife
> If the Lord forgives you, it's all right.

1 Kings 18: 4: And Elijah said unto them, Take the prophets of Baal; let not one of them escape. And they took them: and Elijah brought them down to the brook Kishon, and slew them there.

> Ba'al was one of many gods of the sky.
> At first his thunder would terrify.
> After 1500 years
> He now appears
> As a false god that was evil in God's eye.

2 Kings 1: 10 / 2:8 : And Elijah answered and said to the captain of fifty; If I be a man of God, then let fire come down from heaven, and consume thee and thy fifty. And there came down fire from heaven, and consumed him and his fifty.
And Elijah took his mantle, and wrapped it together, and smote the waters, and they were divided hither and thither, so that they two went over on dry ground

And Elijah had more tricks than David.
There wasn't much that God would forbid.
You may remember when
His fire killed fifty men
And he parted waters like Moses did.

2 Kings 2: 23,24: And he went up from thence unto Bethel: and as he was going up by the way, there came forth little children out of the city, and mocked him, and said, Go up, thou bald head; go up, thou bald head. And he turned back, and looked on them, and cursed them in the name of the Lord. And there came forth two she bears out of the wood, and tore forty and two children of them.

Elijah could not have been worse.
He killed forty-two youths with a curse.
They called him "Bald head"
When they should have said,
"How handsome you are" and in verse.

2 Kings 4: 1,44: Now there cried a certain woman of the wives of the sons of the prophets unto Elisha........So he set it before them, and they did eat, and left thereof, according to the word of the Lord.

Now in 2 Kings Chapter four,
A dead child did Elisha restore.
And oil in a pot

He increased quite a lot.
Read the gospels and find even more.

2 Kings 8: 1: Then spake Elisha unto the woman, whose son he had restored to life, saying, Arise, and go thou and thine household, and sojourn wheresoever thou canst sojourn: for the Lord hath called for a famine; and it shall also come upon the land seven years.

Though famines bring grown men to tears
They only last seven short years.
In Egypt we know
There was one long ago
And now one in Israel appears.

2 Kings 6: 5,6: But as one was felling a beam, the ax head fell into the water: and he cried, and said, Alas, Master! for it was borrowed. And the man of God said, Where fell it? And he shewed him the place. And he cut down a stick, and cast it in thither; and the iron did swim.

Now Harry Houdini did lots of tricks,
And Harry Blackstone knew forty-six.
But Elisha could float
Iron like a boat
When he tossed in a river his sticks.

2 Kings 17: 22,23: For the children of Israel walked in all the sins of Jeroboam which he did; they departed not from them; Until the Lord removed Israel out of his sight, as he had said by all his servants the prophets. So was Israel carried away out of their own land to Assyria unto this day.

Judah and Israel were in accord
They bought all the idols they could afford.
Adrammelech and Baal,

And those were not all.
They were evil in the sight of the Lord.

The books of Kings takes us right up to history when we finally meet records from Babylonian and Assyrian libraries. King Saul we know only from the Bible and "The House of David", inscribed on a basalt stele from ninth century BCE found through excavations on Tel Dan near the Jordan River in northern Israel. This is the only extra-biblical mention of David, although even it is not without its detractors. Below the Temple Mount in Jerusalem lies an immense hall used by Muslims and which has been called "Solomon's Stables", although there is no evidence that Solomon even knew of the hall.

However, when it comes to the conquering of ancient Israel by the Assyrians and their removal of the ten lost tribes of Israel or to the destruction of the first temple in Jerusalem by the Babylonians and the resettlement of thousands of principal leaders of the tribes of Judah and Benjamin, we are on firmer ground because of the records kept by the Assyrians and Babylonians.

The next books, Chronicles I and II, repeat, substantiate or embellish much of what we learned from Samuels and Kings.

1 Chronicles 9: 1: So all Israel was enrolled by genealogies; and these are written in the Book of Kings of Israel. And Judah was taken into exile in Babylon because of their unfaithfulness.

Chronicles are an interesting compilation
Of the people of the Old Hebrew nation,
From Adam and Josiah,
To Jotham and Hezekiah,
And to every old Jewish generation.

1 Chronicles 36: 20 : And them that had escaped from the sword carried he away to Babylon; where they were servants to him and his sons until the reign of the kingdom of Persia.

> The people of Judah were so vile
> That God forsook them after a while.
> In a notable event
> To Babylon they went,
> Spending the rest of their lives in exile.

The authors of Kings and Chronicles listed all the chiefs, prophets, and kings that did evil in the sight of the Lord and ultimately were banished to the cities of the Medes or to become servants to the elite of Babylon.

After an unknown number of years, the lands of Mesopotamia became part of the Persian empire and the famous and benevolent king, Cyrus, allowed those Judeans who had been servants, or sons of servants, to return to Jerusalem and Israel. Some who had assimilated into the Babylonian society chose to remain in Babylonia others, such as Ezra, chose to leave for Judah and a new life among the Judans who continued to be evil in the sight of the Lord.

Ezra returned and chastised the indigenous peoples and has been accused of authoring several books of the 'Old Testament'.

CHAPTER 10

EZRA, NEHEMIAH, ESTHER

The book of Ezra (and possibly the books of the Corinthians) were written by a Levite scribe known as Ezra after he had returned from Babylon. They contain genealogical records of names of those thousands who had preceded or followed him from exile as well as a modicum of history.

The goal of Ezra was to take charge of Judah and Jerusalem. As the new leader he objected to the marriage of the previous returnees to the pagan or gentile members of the indigenous population. He thus commanded that the Jews abandon their gentile wives and children and send them on their way.

On the other hand, Nehemiah's objective was to rebuild the walls of Jerusalem. That project, like the rebuilding of the temple, was interrupted by protests and pleas to whichever king was the ruler at the time.

Ultimately the wall around Jerusalem was completed and houses were built and shops opened.

Esther deserves a separate book because she saved a multitude of Jews from annihilation. And in another example, the sons of Haman, ten in number, were punished for the sins of their father.

Probably because of her beauty and youth, Esther replaced Vashti, also beautiful and fair to look on, as the queen, because Vashti ignored a command of the king.

As the new queen Esther was able to influence the king and earned a place in the Holy Book.

Ezra 2: 64: The whole congregation together was forty and two thousand three hundred and threescore.

> So Cyrus the Great opened the door
> Letting out Judeans, the rich and the poor.
> We can't be too sure
> But off to Judah were
> 42,000 people and maybe some more.

Ezra 7: 6: This Ezra went up from Babylon; and he was a ready scribe in the law of Moses, which the Lord God of Israel had given: and the king granted him all his request, according to the hand of the Lord his God upon him.

> Ezra wasn't much of a fighter
> But few scribes were much brighter.
> He worked to compose
> Much Biblical prose,
> So he's known as a notable writer.

Ezra 8: 1, 9: These are now the chief of their fathers, and this is the genealogy of them that went up with me from Babylon, in the reign of Artaxerxes

Of the sons of Joab; Obadiah the son of Jehiel, and with him two hundred eighteen males.

> What good are biblical tales
> That mention only the males?
> Where are all the girls
> With their cute little curls?
> Checking out the local Bazaar sales?

Ezra 10: 17: And they made an end with all the men that had taken strange wives by the first day of the first month.

> Ezra was like your grand mother
> Who thot you should marry none other
> Than a cousin or aunt,
> But an uncle you can't.
> And don't even consider your brother.

Ezra 10: 1: And they gave their hands that they would put away their wives; and being guilty, they offered a ram of the flock for their trespass.

> Ezra decided way back then,
> You don't marry 'daughters of men'.
> Take Noah's advice
> Marry someone nice
> Like one of God's chosen children.

Nehemiah 1: 2-3: . . . and I asked them concerning the Jews that had escaped, which were left of the captivity, and concerning Jerusalem. And they said unto me, The remnant that are left of the captivity there in the province are in great affliction and reproach: the wall of Jerusalem also is broken down, and the gates thereof are burned with fire.

Nehemiah had heard of the Jews
Who were almost eating their shoes.
The wall was broken down
Around Jerusalem town,
And rubble filled most avenues.

Nehemiah 5: 7, 11: Then I consulted with myself, and I rebuked the nobles, and the rulers, and said unto them, Ye exact usury, every one of his brother. And I set a great assembly against them.
Restore, I pray you, to them, even this day, their lands, their vineyards, their oliveyards, and their houses, also the hundredth part of the money, and of the corn, the wine, and the oil, that ye exact of them.

Early on Jews learned how to trade
And to live off loans that they made.
But then they agreed,
As a kindly good deed,
To consider all debts to be paid.

Nehemiah 7: 6: These are the children of the province, that went up out of the captivity, of those that had been carried away, whom Nebuchadnezzar the king of Babylon had carried away, and came again to Jerusalem and to Judah, every one unto his city.

Forty thousand returned to the homeland
Though few had been there beforehand.
Children of Joab,
And Pahath-Moab
Would live in the Jew's Promised land.

Esther 1: 19: If it please the king, let there go a royal commandment from him, and let it be written among the laws of the Persians and the Medes, that it be not altered. That Vashti come no more before the king

Ahasuerus; and let the king give her royal estate unto another who is better than she.

> Vashti was somewhat chagrined
> When her queenship the king did rescind.
> But employment she sought
> And shortly she got
> A part in 'Gone With the Wind'.

Esther 8: 3: And Esther spake again before the king, and fell down at his feet, and besought him with tears to put away the mischief of Haman the Agagite, and his device that he had devised against the Jews.

> An heroic woman was Esther.
> The fate of the Jews depressed her.
> To the king she appealed
> And caused him to yield.
> God and the Jews then blessed her.

Esther 9: 12,13 : And the king said unto Esther the queen, The Jews have slain and destroyed five hundred men in Shushan the palace, and the ten sons of Haman;
Then said Esther, If it please the king.....let Haman's ten sons be hanged upon the gallows.

> Haman's ten sons were now cold.
> How long they'd been dead we're not told.
> Esther wished them strung up
> Then all ten were hung up
> Ten lifeless bodies on a scaffold.

Ezra is chronologically out of place in the Bible but because of the late date of it's composition it gives us a narrative of the resettling of Jerusalem and the rebuilding of the wall, a task assumed by

Nehemiah, a contemporary of Ezra. When the Persian king Cyrus permitted the Jews to return to Jerusalem and to rebuild the temple he contributed much to the reconstruction such as returning items confiscated by his royal predecessors. Cyrus, it seems, was not of the royal line and therefore may have been more compassionate and understanding than the previous kings.

Many Jews in the world today do not wish to move to Israel because they enjoy a comfortable life in the diaspora. Similarily, many prosperous and comfortable Jews in Babylon elected to remain in Mesopotamia rather than return to an unknown future in Judah.

Fortunately for biblical scholars much of what the prophets of the fifth century BC wrote can be substantiated by records of the Assyrian or Babylonian kings. As with many accounts of historical events, the Biblical accounts may suffer from typographical errors or exaggerations, but for the most part the records of king Cyrus and the records of Ezra are similar and the dating of the former aids in the dating of Ezra and Nehemiah.

Esther may have been a book of fiction that demonstrated what power a Jewish woman can yield as she saved many of her people from annihilation. In subsequent centuries, specifically in the 1940s, it was the gentile women who filled the role of Esther by saving thousands of Jewish women and children from extermination by the Naziis and their collaborators.

CHAPTER 11

JOB, PSALMS AND PROVERBS

This book is the story of the man from the land of Uz, whose name was Job. Since he was probably the most devout follower of the Lord he was the subject of a test. A new character on the scene, the Devil, converses with God. He proposes to weaken Job's faith by destroying his wealth. God approves providing that Job is not touched. Job remains faithful to his Lord, unlike some today who curse their God because he let their child die.

The Devil then suggests that if Job suffers boils, carbuncles, and rashes he will accuse his Lord of abandoning him and curse Him. The Lord agrees but tells the Devil that he cannot cause Job to die.

So the Devil causes boils which afflict Job from head to toe. Job he does not curse his God but, in conversation with three friends, he philosophizes, justifying his faith.

David played his harp and composed some psalms before or during his term as king of Israel. The editors have indicated the psalms of David with the chapter introduction "A Psalm of David". It is assumed that David wrote about half of the 150 psalms.

Solomon, David's son, is credited with many of the proverbs found in the Book of Proverbs. Chapter 1, verse 1 begins 'The proverbs of Solomon son of David, king of Israel' and is reaffirmed in Chapter 10, verse 1.

Any bright saying had to be spoken by Solomon either by memory or through his own composition as he was 'the wisest of men'.

Job 1: 6, 12: Now there was a day when the sons of God came to present themselves before the Lord, and Satan came also among them.
And the Lord said unto Satan, Behold, all that he hath is in thy power; only upon himself put not forth thy hand. So Satan went forth from the presence of the Lord.

> In the Holy Bible, Act Five.
> Finally old Satan does arrive,
> Shortly to begin
> To incite Job to sin,
> But God makes sure Job stays alive.

Job 41: 19-21: Out of his mouth go burning lamps, and sparks of fire leap out....Out of his nostrils goeth smoke, as out of a seething pot or caldron ....His breath kindleth coals, and a flame goeth out of his mouth.

> God lists the powers of leviathan.
> In size he was second to none.
> He exhaled fire
> Which you must admire.
> He reminds me of a Chinese dragon.

I Samuel 16: 17,18: And Saul said unto his servants, Provide me now a man that can play well, and bring him to me. Then answered one of the servants, and said, Behold, I have seen a son of Jesse the Bethlehemite, that is cunning in playing, and a mighty valiant man, and a man of war, and prudent in manners.........

> Elvis, Caruso and Louie Armstrong
> Made a good living with their song.
> David chose to be king
> Rather than to only sing.
> Of course, again, I could be wrong.

Psalms 23: 6: Surely goodness and mercy shall follow me all the days of my life: and I will dwell in the house of the Lord for ever.

> A favorite psalm for me and thee,
> Is the one numbered twenty-three.
> The Lord by my side
> He shall be my guide.
> Goodness and mercy shall follow me.

Psalms 100: 1- 3: Make a joyful noise unto the Lord, all ye lands. Serve the Lord with gladness: come before his presence with singing. Know ye that the Lord he is God; it is he that hath made us, and not we ourselves; we are his people, and the sheep of his pasture.

> Make a joyful noise, all the lands.
> God hath made us, with his hands.
> He shows his love
> From far above
> And ignores our most inane demands.

Psalms 146-150: Praise ye the Lord. Praise the Lord, O my soul. Praise ye the Lord; for it is good to sing praises unto our God; Praise ye the Lord. Praise ye the Lord from the heavens. Praise ye the Lord. Sing unto the Lord a new song. Praise ye the Lord. Praise God in his sanctuary;

David's love, his psalm conveys,
And we pay homage on Holidays.
We tend to state
That God is great.
Like David's psalms, we sing our praise.

Proverbs 1: 7: The fear of the Lord is the beginning of knowledge: but fools despise wisdom and instruction.

It pays to heed King Solomon's words
Though they don't sound pretty like birds.
They're full of advice
At a reasonable price
And good reading for many shep herds.

Proverbs 10: 1: The proverbs of Solomon. A wise son maketh a glad father: but a foolish son is the heaviness of his mother.

King Solomon had the knack,
To write proverbs, that others lack.
Like early to rise
Makes one wise.
Or was that Poor Richard's Almanac?

Proverbs 20: 29: The glory of young men is their strength: and the beauty of old men is the gray head.

Which of the proverbs is the best?
Is there one standing out from the rest?
Some are real great
I know at least eight.
Is there one that you would suggest?

Proverbs 21: 9 / 21: 19 / 25: 24: It is better to dwell in the corner of the housetop, than with a brawling woman in a wide house.
It is better to dwell in the wilderness, than with a contentious and angry woman.
It is better to dwell in the corner of the housetop, than with a brawling woman and in a wide house.

> Chapter 25: 24 is a copy of Solomon
> About a contentious and angry person.
> It's different in style
> Might make you smile,
> Unless you're a brawling old woman.

Job is such a sad story that I don't even want to think about it. Psalms on the other hand has memorable verses some of which I remember even the 23d Psalm in French which begins something like 'L'Eternal est mon berger'. My favorite Psalm was the 100th which, probably because of its length (short) I also memorized as a youth.

The proverbs of Solomon provides more advice than Benjamin Franklin in Poor Richards Almanac, but Solomon focused on good and evil and the value of instruction over ignorance.

I don't recall if the proverbs mentioned the advantages of going to bed early and rising early (Franklin's formula for gaining wisdom) but Solomon tells us that "The fear of the Lord is the beginning of knowledge; but fools despise wisdom and instruction."

CHAPTER 12

ECCLESIASTES
SONG OF SOLOMON
ISAIAH

The book of Ecclesiastes was written by or for the son of David who was king in Jerusalem. That could have been Solomon who was deemed the wisest of men. However, since it may have been written much later than the time of King Solomon, many scholars question the authorship. Students of the Bible also wonder why such a pessimistic book should be included in the Bible in the first place. The reason may be that it separates the proverbs of Solomon from the Song of Solomon. Of course you may come up with a better reason.

Isaiah was a major prophet who, like many others, spoke for the Lord, passing on His message which usually consisted of predictions of what would happen if the people of Israel continued on their evil ways.

Adam and Eve may have been the first of those with free will to transgress but throughout the 'Old Testament' scribes, prophets and kings warned the people not to do evil in the sight of the Lord because worshipping idols, Baal, or other false gods will engender God's wrath and cause disaster.

Ecclesiastes 1: 7: All the rivers run into the sea; yet the sea is not full; unto the place from whence the rivers come, thither they return again.

> Most rivers run to the sea.
> Then it rains on you and on me.
> It was God's plan
> Since time began
> To water the earth for me and thee.

Song of Solomon 4: 1: Behold, thou art fair, my love; behold, thou art fair; thou hast doves eyes within thy locks: thy hair is as a flock of goats, that appear from mount Gilead.

> Solomon could really turn a phrase
> He was a composer from the early days.
> To cite a sample
> As an example
> 'go about the city, and in the broad ways'.

Isaiah 1: 1: The vision of Isaiah the son of Amoz, which he saw concerning Judah and Jerusalem in the days of Uzziah, Jotham, Ahaz, and Hezekiah, kings of Judah.

> A Prophet, Isaiah by name,
> Was not in it for fame.
> He heard from his Lord
> And recalled every word
> And thus a true prophet became.

Isaiah 2: 1: The word that Isaiah the son of Amoz saw concerning Judah and Jerusalem.

Some prophets were better than others.
We know their fathers, not their mothe.
From God they all heard
And passed on His word
From Our God, not from another's.

Isaiah 2: 8: Their land also is full of idols; they worship the work of their own hands, that which their own fingers have made.

Ye whose idols fill all your lands,
Who worship things made by your hands.
Forsake your evil ways
Hear what Isaiah says
Accede to what the Lord God demands.

Isaiah 3: 16: Moreover the Lord saith, Because the daughters of Zion are haughty, and walk with stretched forth necks and wanton eyes, walking and mincing as they go, and making a tinkling with their feet.

Women of Jerusalem, beware.
Ye may real soon lose your hair.
Your mincing walk,
Your haughty talk,
May be acceptable elsewhere.

Isaiah 4: 5: And the Lord will create upon every dwelling place of mount Zion, and upon her assemblies, a cloud and smoke by day, and the shining of a flaming fire by night: for upon all the glory shall be a defence.

We've had prophets, good and bad.
Isaiah is the best we've ever had.
He could prophesy

In the blink of an eye.
He was even well known in Bagdad.

Isaiah 5: 11: Woe unto them that rise up early in the morning, that they may follow strong drink; that continue unto night, til wine inflame them.

God told Isaiah to announce
That every good deed really counts.
In the eternal quest
To join the blessed,
And the use of strong drink, renounce.

Isaiah 6: 6,7: Then flew one of the seraphims unto me, having a live coal in his hand, which he had taken with the tongs from off the alter:

I can not imagine a Jew
Misspelling Seraphim, can you?
In King James' Version,
Says Daniel Gershon,
Seraphim means at least two.

Isaiah 8: 1: Moreover the Lord said unto me, Take thee a great roll, and write in it with a man's pen concerning Mahershalalhashbaz.

Reading Isaiah 8 made me think
Was it ballpoint, gel or just ink?
Did they have pens?
And were they just man's?
And does octopus ink contain zinc?

Isaiah 11: 6: The wolf shall dwell with the lamb and the leopard shall lie down with the kid, and the calf and the young lion and the fatling together; and a little child shall lead them.

If the vegans have their own way
Everything shall eschew meat someday.
And time will pass
As everything eats grass,
And the calves, cubs, and kids will go play.

Isaiah 24: 1: Behold, the Lord maketh the earth empty, and maketh it waste, and turneth it upside down, and scattereth abroad the inhabitants thereof.

In Isaiah God mentions desolation,
Of not just one, but every nation.
Except for Armageddon
And an occasional dragon,
It reminds me a lot like "Revelation".

CHAPTER 13

JEREMIAH
LAMENTATIONS OF JEREMIAH
EZEKIEL

The works of the prophet Jeremiah are convoluted and confusing but his so-called prophesy contains some history from before the exile, during and after. Also, like other prophets, major or minor, quoting God, he warns the people of the consequences of disloyalty and lack of faith. Jeremiah also informs the people that God has 'set' him over nations and over kingdoms. Few prophets have been granted that much power.

The Lamentation of Jeremiah allows us to witness the sorrow of 'the daughter if Zion', the city of Jerusalem, when she was abandoned and desecrated. The city does admit that she, and her people, had been evil in the sight of the Lord and therefore merited her punishment; the exile of her nobles and the destruction of Jerusalem and Judah.

Jeremiah 1: 9,10 : Then the Lord put forth his hand and touched my mouth; and the Lord said to me, "Behold, I have put my words in your mouth......See, I have set you this day over nations and over kingdoms, to pluck up and to break down, to destroy and to overthrow, to build and to plant."

Jeremiah also, the Lord's voice heard.
And he was charged to pass on His word.
Though temporary,
Like a canary,
He was granted the power of the Lord.

Jeremiah 32: 29: And the Chaldeans, that fight against this city shall come and set fire on this city, and burn it with the houses, upon whose roofs they have offered incense unto Baal, and poured out drink offerings unto other gods, to provoke me to anger.

Murder and torture may be scary
But to God they were secondary.
What made him sad,
Or excessively mad,
Was your attending a Ba'al seminary.

Lamentations of Jeremiah. 4: 12: The kings of the earth, and all the inhabitants of the world, would not have believed that the adversary and the enemy should have entered into the gates of Jerusalem.

Lamentations is an appropriate word
Of greater misery we haven't heard.
So much moaning,
Crying, and groaning.
Excess wailing over Jerusalem is absurd.

Ezekiel 1: 5,6 Also out of the midst thereof came the likeness of four living creatures. And this was their appearance; they had a likeness of man. And every one had four faces, and every one had four wings.

Ezekiel saw four things with four wings.
Evidently he was seeing things.
He also saw a wheel

But it wasn't real
It's what too much hard liquor brings.

Ezekiel 3: 3: And he said unto me, Son of man, cause thy belly to eat, and fill thy bowels with this roll that I give thee. Then did I eat it; and it was in my mouth as honey for sweetness.

Why did the Lord God suggest
That Ezekiel, the priest, should injest
A written scroll
(An inscribed roll)?
Maybe the document was blessed.

Ezekiel 7: 15: The sword is without, and the pestilence and the famine within: he that is in the field shall die with the sword; and he that is in the city, famine and pestilence shall devour him.

Ezekiel like other forecasters
Predicted many disasters.
But to be fair
He wasn't there
Don't quote him, you rabbis and pastors.

Ezekiel 18: 5, 8: But if a man be just, and do that which is lawful and right. He that hath not given forth upon usury, neither hath taken any increase, that hath withdrawn his hand from iniquity, hath executed true judgment between man and man.

It's ironic what Ezekiel says
Since Jews for thousands of days
Could only lend money
Which seems rather funny
They couldn't make money other ways.

Ezekiel 20: 41,42: I will accept you with your sweet savor, when I bring you out from the people, and gather you out of the countries wherein ye have been scattered; and I will be sanctified in you before the heathen. And ye shall know that I am the Lord, when I shall bring you into the land of Israel, into the country for which I lifted up mine hand to give it to your fathers.

Is Israel's motto known to you?
Is it Ezekiel Twenty, Forty-two?
Jews would come home
From wherever they did roam.
Did Ezekiel predict that event, too?

Ezekiel 21: 2,3: Son of man, set thy face toward Jerusalem, and drop thy sword toward the holy places, and prophesy against the land of Israel, And say to the land of Israel, Thus saith the Lord; Behold I am against thee, and will draw forth my sword out of his sheath, and will cut off from thee the righteous and the wicked.

Ezekiel the prophet once said
That evil doers would all be dead.
But he wasn't sure
That it would occur.
Bless his Judean bald head.

Ezekiel 29: 9,10: And the land of Egypt shall be desolate and waste; and they shall know that I am the Lord: because he hath said, The river is mine, and I have made it.
Behold, therefore I am against thee, and against thy rivers, and I will make the land of Egypt utterly waste and desolate, from the tower of Syene even to the border of Ethiopia

Ezekiel as a prophet was good.
God told him more than he should.

Egypt, he forecast,
Would be a thing of the past.
But he did no better than you would.

It is Jewish tradition that Jeremiah was the author of the Book of Kings, the Book of Lamentations, and, of course, the Book of Jeremiah. He was condemned for his pessimistic prophesies of Jerusalem's destruction and was imprisoned by the officials of the government of king Zedekiah until the conquering Babylonians freed him and honored him. He later sought exile in the land of Egypt.

Ezekiel, along with Isaiah and Jeremiah, was one of the three major prophets. He is another biblical character who incorporates that old Sumerian god, El, in his name. Ezekiel is translated as 'strengthened by God'. Ezekiel, the prophet, condemned Judah for doing evil in the sight of the Lord. His later prophesies indicated a revival of the nations of Israel and Judah and a return to the fold of the Israelite God.

CHAPTER 14

DANIEL
HOSEA
JOEL

Sometimes, as when he renamed Jacob, God chose names for his favorites, but if it weren't for the head eunuch in Nebuchadnezzar's court we would never have heard of Shadrach, Meshach or Abednego. Daniel was also renamed by the king's eunuch but Belteshazzar didn't stick. Thus we have the book of Daniel.

The story of Daniel in the lion's den is not great drama but it may have been included to demonstrate how the angels of God earn their keep. Or it may have been to show the king just who he is messing with besides Daniel; his God and the angels.

While it is possible that most prophets could interpret dreams, we know of Joseph and of Daniel. The prophets could also understand their own dreams and visions while entranced. A more modern prophet was Edgar Cayce who could diagnose health problems and offer remedies, also while in a self-imposed hypnotic state. His prophesies also proved valid.

Hosea was a minor prophet in that his writings, as were those of the other 11 minor prophets, short and sweet. Quite frequently the prophets use allegory or metaphor to express their point which can be rather frustrating, but provides work for biblical scholars.

Joel reports that God will bring his people together and will judge those who have abused them.

Daniel 1:16: Thus Melzar took away the portion of their meat, and the wine that they should drink; and gave them pulse.

> Was Daniel paid by the vegans
> To eat only vegetables and brans?
> He sure looked good
> After eating vegan food,
> But still didn't join the vegetarians.

Daniel 3: 23, 25: And these three men, Shadrach, Meshach, and Abednego, fell down bound into the midst of the burning fiery furnace.…. He answered and said, Lo, I see four men loose, walking in the midst of the fire, and they have no hurt; and the form of the fourth is like the Son of God.

> Shadrach engendered the king's ire
> Who forced him and friends into fire.
> They weren't worn-out
> When they walked out.
> They didn't even seem to perspire.

Daniel 4: 18: This dream I king Nebuchadnezzar have seen. Now thou, O Belteshazzar, declare the interpretation thereof, forasmuch as all the wise men of my kingdom are not able to make known unto me the interpretation: but thou art able; for the spirit of the holy gods is in thee.

Remember Joseph long ago,
Who interpreted dreams of pharaoh?
Now Daniel it seems
Also knows dreams.
If he's wrong, who is to know?

Daniel 6: 16: Then the king commanded, and they brought Daniel, and cast him into the den of lions. Now the king spake and said unto Daniel, Thy God whom thou servest continually, he will deliver thee.

You know Daniel in the lion's den.
He was shut in by the king's men.
God's angels came around
And the lion's mouths bound.
The animals were much tamer then.

Hosea 2: 4: And I will not have mercy upon her children; for they be the children of whoredoms.

God disliked innocent infants
Whether wearing dresses or pants.
If their mom was unfit,
Caring for kids not a bit.
Those kids weren't given a chance.

Hosea 11: 1,2: When Israel was a child, then I loved him, and called my own out of Egypt.
As they called them, so they went from them: they sacrificed unto Baalim, and burned incense to graven images.

They praised storm gods and the sun.
Then they sacrificed unto only one
The Creator of all

Or the storm god Ba'al.
Today quite a few worship none.

Joel 1: 1: The word of the Lord that came to Joel son of Pethuel.

If your name isn't Rachel or Joel
But Frank or Willie or Noel.
You might not be Jewish
But you still could wish
That God would save your dear soul.

Joel 1: 15: Alas for the day! For the day of the Lord is near, and as destruction from the Almighty it comes.

Joel reads like 'Revelation'.
He writes of fire and desolation.
He also speaks
Of the invading Greeks,
And then Judah's final vindication.

Daniel as a Book or as a prophet seems in limbo since it does not appear in the Jewish canon as a prophet and was evidently written as late as 165 BCE.

Still, we have the enduring story of Daniel in the lion's den along with a few visions that he had concerning kings and empires.

Daniel appears in this chapter because it is the order in which the editors of the canon chose. It is appropriate that the book of Daniel appears between the book of Ezekiel, a major prophet, and Hosea, a minor prophet. We can refer to him as a medium prophet.

To give chapter 14 more substance we have included the first two minor prophets, Hosea and Joel. The other ten minor prophets may have been common men or shepherds as was Amos but in many cases we are introduced to their fathers and even grandfathers. As a group they tend to see the iniquities of the people and the punishments God will inflict upon them unless they return to the fold; keeping God's commandments and forsaking foreign gods and idols.

CHAPTER 15

AMOS OBADIAH JONAH MICAH NAHUM HABAKKUK ZEPHANIAH HAGGAI ZECHARIAH MALACHI

It was not necessary to be of the nobility to become a prophet. Amos was a shepherd and the other minor prophets are evidently not high on the social scale or they would have mentioned it. All that was necessary was the ability to remember and record all visions that appeared to them while in a trance or deep sleep.

The visions of the minor prophets were so similar and so confusing that modern rabbis, priests and pastors tend to avoid mentioning them in their sermons.

Fortunately the twelve lessor or minor prophets are included in the last part of the Old Testament and in at least in some cases were written after the events which the prophets prophesy. That maybe why Nahum is so ecstatic about the destruction of Nineveh by the Chaldeans (Babylonians), although, at the time of his prophesy, the destruction may only have been imminent.

Amos 7: 17: Therefore thus saith the Lord; Thy wife shall be an harlot in the city, and thy sons and thy daughters shall fall by the sword, and thy land shall be divided by line; and thou shalt die in a polluted land: and Israel shall surely go into captivity forth of his land.

> I do not think you can blame us
> If certain Bible books are not famous.
> Some are a blessing
> Others depressing,
> Like God's warnings delivered by Amos.

Amos 9: 14,15: And I will bring again the captivity of my people of Israel, and they shall build the waste cities, and inhabit them; and they shall plant vineyards, and drink the wine thereof; they shall also make gardens, and eat the fruit of them. And I will plant them upon their land, and they shall no more be pulled out of their land which I have given them, saith the Lord thy God.

> God wants you to understand
> He'll bring Jews back to their land.
> Not right away
> But some sunny day
> When they obey the good Lord's command.

Obadiah 1: 20: And the captivity of this host of the children of Israel shall possess that of the Canaanites, even unto Zarephath; and the captivity of Jerusalem, which is in Sepharad, shall possess the cities of the south.

> Obadiah had a thing about Edom
> But he prophesied about Israelite freedom.
> It all came to pass
> Except one thing, alas,
> Their homes; the Israelites won't need'em.

Jonah 1: 17 : Now the Lord had prepared a great fish to swallow up Jonah. And Jonah was in the belly of the fish three days and three nights.

> You've heard of Jonah and the whale
> That God made just for this tale.
> According to the plan
> It was built so a man
> Could walk from its head to its tail.

Micah 2: 6: Prophesy ye not, say they to them that prophesy: they shall not prophesy to them, that they shall not take shame.

> False prophets may have existed,
> Though their prophesies never are listed.
> We did our best
> And sort of guessed
> Of what they probably consisted.

Nahum 1: 1: The burden of Nineveh. The book of the vision of Nahum the Elkoshite.

> Nahum had a one track mind
> His prophesies were one of a kind
> Ninevah will be crushed
> Its streets full of dust.
> The Chaldeans will leave nothing behind.

Nahum 3: 7: And it shall come to pass, that all they that look upon thee shall flee from thee, and say, Nineveh is laid waste: who will bemoan her? whence shall I seek comforters for thee?

> Nineveh's demise was regrettable
> But t'was an event that is forgettable.
> Does anyone care

What went on over there?
Back when clams and pork were inedible.

Habakkuk 3: 2: O Lord, I have heard thy speech, and was afraid: O Lord, revive thy work in the midst of the years, in the midst of the years make known; in wrath remember mercy.

There once was a prophet, Habakkuk,
Who saw evil wherever he'd look.
He knelt down in prayer,
It's all written there
In his short little Habakkuk book.

Zephaniah 1: 2,3: I will utterly consume all things from off the land, saith the Lord......I will consume man and beast; I will consume the fowls of the heaven, and the fishes of the sea, and the stumbling blocks with the wicked; and I will cut off man from off the land, saith the Lord.

The Lord again made a threat
Which hasn't been carried out yet.
He promised at least
To kill man and beast
But, unlike with Noah, did He forget?

Haggai 1: 14: And the Lord stirred up the spirit of Zerubbabel the son of Shealtiel, governor of Judah, and the spirit of Joshua the son of Josedech, the high priest, and the spirit of all the remnant of the people; and they came and did work in the house of the Lord of hosts, their God.

The Lord told the prophet Haggai
The governor and the people, notify.
That with stones and with board

Rebuild the house of the Lord
And thus, the Lord of hosts, mollify.

Zechariah 14: 2: For I will gather all nations against Jerusalem to battle; and the city shall be taken, and the houses rifled, and the women ravished; and half the city shall go forth into captivity, and the residue of the people shall not be cut off from the city.

Zechariah died long ago
But he prophesied tales of woe,
Of cities burnt down,
Of deaths in a town,
It was God who told him, you know.

Malachi 4: 1: FOR, behold, the day cometh, that shall burn as an oven; and all the proud, yea, and all that do wickedly, shall be stubble: and the day that cometh shall burn them up, saith the Lord of hosts, that it shall leave them neither root nor branch.

The Old Testament's a little too long.
It should end with Solomon's song.
Or maybe with Micah,
Or Jeremiah.
Maybe even those don't belong.

NEW
TESTAMENT

CHAPTER 1

MATTHEW

Matthew, the first of the four gospels, was originally written for Jews who lived around Syria and the Sea of Galilee. The author lists the genealogy of Jesus as well as His short history from birth to death and resurrection. Furthermore, in Matthew is recorded the words of Jesus known as the 'Sermon on the Mount' and recounts a collection of miracles, healings and parables. Originally Jesus instructed his disciples, to whom He had granted the power to perform miracles, to preach only among the Jews but later, upon his resurrection, directed his disciples to 'teach all nations, baptizing them in the name of the Father, and of the Son, and of the Holy Spirit'.

Matthew 1: 17: So all the generations from Abraham to David are fourteen generations; and from David until the carrying away into Babylon are fourteen generations; and from the carrying away into Babylon unto Christ are fourteen generations.

> Christ's ancestors were Rehoboam
> David, Solomon and Esrom.
> Forty-two generations
> From several nations
> Thanks to Ancestry dot com.

Matthew 2: 1: 1 And when they were come into the house, they saw the young child . . . they presented unto him gifts: gold, and frankincense, and myrrh.

> It seems that when Mary gave birth
> A bright star shown down on earth,
> And three men did appear
> Near the end of the year.
> I wonder what Frankincense was worth.

Matthew 1: 1 / 28: 20: The book of the genealogy of Jesus Christ, the son of David, the son of Abraham - - . . and, lo, I am with you always, even unto the end of the world. Amen.

> According to Matthew's own story
> Jesus was destined for glory.
> And throughout his life
> He didn't find a wife.
> Of that he never seemed sorry.

Matthew 2: 1,2: Now when Jesus was born in Bethlehem of Judea in the days of Herod, the king, behold, there came wise men from the east to Jerusalem, saying, Where is he that is born "King of the Jews? For we have seen his star in the east, and are come to worship him.

> From the East wise men appeared,
> Some clean shaven, some with a beard.
> They brought myrrh and gold
> And what I've been told
> Their speech seemed rather weird.

Matthew 2: 16: Then Herod. . . was exceedingly angry, and sent forth, and slew all the children that were in Bethlehem, and in all its borders, from two years old and under . . .

Herod the Great was rather cruel.
Great men don't kill kids as a rule.
But he sent out a crew
To kill kids under two.
Did you read of that while in school?

Matthew 5: 1-2 / 7: 28 : And seeing the multitudes, he went up into a mountain: and when he was seated, his disciples came unto him. And he opened his mouth, and taught them, saying, . .
And it came to pass, when Jesus had ended these sayings, the people were astonished at his doctrine;

If you seek some good advice
Finding one source would be nice.
The gospel of Matthew
Provides thirty-two
Though thirty-one would suffice.

Matthew 5:5/11:28: Blessed are the meek; for they shall inherit the earth....Come unto me, all ye that labor and are heavy laden, and I will give you rest.

In Christ's sermon is the Lord's Prayer
That's not all that we locate in there
Christ blessed the meek
Helped find what ye seek
And lessened the burdens ye bear.

Matthew 8: 1 / 9: 35: When he was come down from the mountain, great multitudes followed him. . . .And Jesus went about all the cities and villages, teaching in their synagogues, and preaching the gospel of the kingdom, and healing every sickness and every disease among the people.

Christ from the mount then descended.
You'd think that his mission had ended.
But in spite what you've heard
He found and he cured
More diseases than he had intended.

Matthew 9: 9: And as Jesus passed forth from there, he saw a man, named Matthew, sitting at the tax office; and he said unto him, Follow me. And he arose, and followed him.

The very first gospel is Matthew.
That's something you already knew.
How old was he
Twenty or seventy three?
Of that we haven't a clue.

Matthew 10: 1: And when he had called unto him his twelve disciples, he gave them power against unclean spirits, to cast them out, and to heal all manner of sickness and all manner of disease.

Does the unique power to cure
Over the centuries still endure?
Do the healers today
Frequently display
The power to heal the impure?

Matthew 11: 4,5: Jesus answered and said unto them, Go and show John again those things which ye do hear and see:
The blind receive their sight, and the lame walk, the lepers are cleansed, and the deaf hear, the dead are raised up, and the poor have the gospel preached unto them.

Jesus gained most of his fame
From things that established his name,

Like curing the sick
And performing the trick
Raising the dead and healing the lame.

Matthew 13: 3-8: And he spoke many things unto them in parables, saying, Behold, a sower went forth to sow . . .And when he sowed, some of the seeds fell by the wayside. . . Some fell on stony places . . some fell among thorns; . . .But other seeds fell into good ground, and brought forth fruit . . .

Some parables you've surely heard
But your memory may be blurred.
Jesus was a teacher
And sometimes a preacher.
Through parable he spread the Word.

Matthew 14: 16-17/ 15: 34: But Jesus said unto them, They need not depart; give them to eat. And they say unto him, We have here but five loaves, and two fishes. . . .
And Jesus saith unto them, How many loaves have ye? And they said, Seven, and a few little fishes.

Christ fed the multitude twice
Loaves and fish; not lamb and rice.
Several thousand, I think
But what did they drink?
A gallon of wine would be nice.

Matthew 8: 20 / 16: 11,12: . . .the Son of man hath not where to lay his head. I spoke not to you concerning bread, Then understood they that he bade them not to beware of leaven bread, but of the doctrine of the Pharisees and the Sadducees.

The Pharisees made leavened bread.
Christ listed other problems instead.
Their doctrine he thought
Was not what he taught,
And he had nowhere to lay his head.

Matthew 19: 24: And again I say unto you, It is easier for a camel to go through the eye of a needle than for a rich man to enter into the kingdom of God.

How big is a needle's eye?
How wealthy is a rich guy?
Is he rich with a million?
How about a billion?
Many men are richer than I.

Matthew 19: 30 : But many that are first shall be last; and the last shall be first. . . Matthew 20: 16:. . . Mark 10: 31:. . .
Luke 13: 30: And behold, there are last which shall be first, and there are first which shall be last.

Jesus gave advice when he dined
Especially after he had wined.
The last would be first
And when that's reversed,
The first would be somewhere behind.

Matthew 23: 13, 29: But woe unto you, scribes and Pharisees, hypocrites! for ye shut up the kingdom of heaven against men. . . . Woe unto you, scribes and Pharisees, hypocrites! because ye build the tombs of prophets, ...

Christ must have had some bad press.
Were scribes envious of his success?

'Hypocrites' was the word
The disciples often heard
When Pharisees Christ would address.

*Matthew 26: 24: The Son of man goeth as it is written of him; but woe
unto that man by whom the Son of man is betrayed!*

The Bible foretold Jesus' fate
But it did not reveal the date.
It would happen soon
Maybe before noon.
That's the closest they could calculate.

*Matthew 26: 25, 33,34: Then Judas, who betrayed him, answered and
said, Master, is it I? He said unto him, Thou hast said. Peter answered
and said unto him, . . yet will I never be offended. Jesus said unto him,
Verily I say unto thee that this night, before the cock crows, thou shalt
deny me thrice.*

The Lord Jesus Christ somehow knew
Which would betray him and who
Would deny him thrice.
Neither would be nice.
Were they worse than me or you?

*Matthew 26: 38,39: Then saith he unto them . . . tarry here, and
watch with me. And he went a little further, and fell on his face, and
prayed, saying, O my Father, if it be possible, let this cup pass from me;
nevertheless, not as I will, but as thou wilt.*

Three disciples of Jesus stayed behind
As he went on forward to find
A quiet vacant place

To fall on his face
And ask God to please change his mind.

Matthew 26: 51: And, behold, one of those who were with Jesus stretched out his hand, and drew his sword, and struck a servant of the high priest's, and smote off his ear. Mark. 14: 47 Luke. 22: 50,5. And one of them smote the servant of the high priest, and cut off his right ear. And Jesus answered, and said, Permit ye thus far. And he touched his ear and healed him

What was Christ's associate thinking?
Maybe he had been drinking
A man that was near
He cut off his ear,
Which Jesus restored without blinking.

Matthew 27: 32: And as they came out, they found a man of Cyrene, Simon by name ; him they compelled to bear his cross.

Have you heard of Simon from Cyrene?
He's someone you've probably not seen
It may be our loss
But does he carry the cross?
Or is it Jesus we see on the screen?

CHAPTER 2

MARK, LUKE, AND JOHN

The gospel of Mark was written with the inhabitants of the Roman Empire in mind. Some believe it is dated about 20 years after Matthew wrote his travelogue, and it is possible that Mark was familiar with Matthew's writings since much of Mark's text duplicates that of Matthew. There are those who believe that the gospel of Mark was written before Matthew but, since Matthew appears first in the New Testament, we shall recognize its priority. It is for this reason we have not turned much of the Gospel of Mark into limericks. In the Gospel of Luke we find even less similarity to Matthew but enough that the first three gospels have been called 'the Synoptic Gospels'. John, on the other hand presents much more original material than the synoptics.

John was one of Christ's disciples but may not have written the gospel bearing his name. Most of the books of the New Testament were written by others than the subject of the book. Since John was one of the twelve disciples he would have been at least 20 when Christ was crucified and seventy or eighty when the gospel of John was written. But it is the content of the Gospel that is important, not the author.

Mark 1: 8: I, indeed, have baptized you with water. Matthew. 3: 11: I . . baptize you with water. Luke. 3: 16: John answered . . . I indeed baptize you with water . . . . John. 1: 26: John . . . saying, I baptize with water. . .

Many verses were stolen from Matthew.
Luke and John stole just a few.
Then there was Mark
Who just for a lark
Stole about a hundred twenty-two.

Mark 8: 13, 22: And he left them, and getting into the boat again, departed to the other side.
And they came to Bethsaida. And some people brought to him a blind man, and begged him to touch him.

Christ, in a boat, left Galilee
And found a man who couldn't see.
Some spit he applied
Then touches he tried
And the man saw better than thee.

Mark 14: 56 / 15: 3: For many bore false witness against him, . . .And the chief priests accused him of many things; but he answered nothing.

It seems Christ never testified.
Most witnesses against him had lied.
Though he held his peace
Lies would never cease,
And Lord Jesus Christ was crucified.

Mark 15: 2: 5 And it was the third hour; and they crucified him

No electricity or injections in those days
They dispatched the guilty in other ways.

And suffer, you must
It may not be just
But crucifixion was all the craze.

Luke 2: 15,16: . . . . the shepherds said one to another, Let us now go even unto Bethlehem, and see this thing which is come to pass,. And they came with haste, and found Mary, and Joseph, and the babe lying in a manger.

If you produce a Christmas play
Check out Luke Two right away.
There's Joseph and Mary,
A shepherd named Jerry,
And a baby asleep on the hay.

Luke 2: 2: And when eight days were accomplished for the circumcising of the child, his name was called Jesus, who was so named by the angel before he was conceived in the womb.

Most babies are usually adored,
Some named before cutting the cord.
It was an angel
That named Ishmael
Another that named Jesus our Lord.

Luke 8: 55, 56: . . she arose straightaway; . . And her parents were amazed; but he charges them that they should tell no man what was done. Luke. 9: 42, 43 And Jesus. .healed the child, .And they were all astonished at the mighty power of God . . .

Jesus seldom expressed much emotion
And wasn't much for self-promotion.
In crowds, many were cured

Others said not a word
A sign of their deep devotion.

John 3: 16 / John 11: 35: For God so loved the world, that he gave his
only begotten son, that whosoever believeth in him should not perish,
but have everlasting life.
Jesus wept.

Some verses we always remember
Whether in September or November.
"Jesus wept", we mean,
Or John: three sixteen.
You'll hear that on 25 December.

John 5: 8,9: Jesus saith unto him, Rise, take up thy bed, and walk.
And immediately the man was made well, and took up his bed and
walked; and the same day was the sabbath.

Christ's healings created a sensation
Though he healed in only one nation.
In Judea and Galilee
Christ cured people free.
Now we have hospitalization.

John 6: 53: So Jesus said unto them, Verily, verily, I say unto you, Except
ye eat of the flesh of the Son of man, and drink his blood, ye have no
life in you.

Jesus changed water into wine,
Just as good as that from the vine.
And now you could
Change wine into blood
When you get in a Communion line.

John 11: 35: Jesus wept.

> Back when you went to Bible School
> Memorizing verses was the rule.
> Many verses filled your head
> "Jesus wept", someone said.
> Reciting that one was always cool.

John 14: 6: Jesus saith unto him, I am the way, and truth, and the life; no man cometh unto the Father, but by me.

> To find the way and the truth
> You won't find it in the Book of Ruth.
> John provides a clue
> Designed to guide you
> To the Father, if you're aged or youth.

John 18: 17, 25, 27: Then saith the maid that kept the door unto Peter, Art not thou also one of this man's disciples? He saith, I am not.

> You know Doubting Thomas, I'm sure.
> His fame will most likely endure.
> And Peter had lied
> When thrice he denied
> Knowing Christ or his ability to cure.

CHAPTER 3

THE ACTS OF THE APOSTLES

Evidently Acts was composed by Luke, the doctor, as a continuation of his gospel. In the first chapter he relates that Christ, after 40 days following his resurrection, was taken up in a cloud as that was the abode of many gods of antiquity - from 2348 B.C.E. - such as Enlil, Marduk, Ba'al, Indra, Zeus, Set, and Thor, to name a few.

As the title implies, Acts records the activities of the Apostles after the death of Jesus, including his 40 days on earth after his resurrection. Although directed by Luke the main character in Acts is Peter, and on that 'rock' was built the church.

Acts 1: 14 : These all continued with one accord in prayer and supplication, with the women, and Mary, the mother of Jesus, and with his brethren.

> Jesus may have had brothers like James.
> The others? I don't know their names.
> But one Bible scholar
> Would bet many a dollar
> They were cousins, or so he exclaims.

Acts 3: 14: But you denied the Holy and Righteous One, and asked for a murderer to be granted to you, . .

> Peter, who denied Jesus thrice
> Told the people of Christ's sacrifice.
> They chose Barabas
> Rather than Jesus
> And Jesus paid the ultimate price.

Acts 5: 30: The God of our fathers raised up Jesus, whom ye slew and hanged on a tree. Acts. 10: 39: . . . whom they slew and hanged on a tree . . .
Acts. 13: 29: . . .they took him down from the tree, and laid him in a sepulcher.

> Many believe Christ was crucified
> But maybe the apostles had lied.
> Was Peter deceived
> When he believed
> Jesus was hanged on a tree when he died.

Acts 5: 19,20: But an angel of the Lord by night opened the prison doors, and brought them forth and said, Go, stand and speak in the temple to the people all the words of this life.

> God's angels have no problem with locks.
> They cure diseases better than docs.
> Most angels are mute
> But that we can dispute
> The angel in Acts 5:20 clearly talks.

Acts 15: 24: Forasmuch as we have heard, that certain which went out from us have troubled you with words, subverting your souls, saying, ye must be circumcised, and keep the law: to whom we gave no such commandment.

> The discussion turned to circumcision
> And Peter and friends made a decision.
> They kept the laws of Moses
> And all that he proposes,
> But Gentiles may skip that incision.

Acts 1: 23: And they appointed two, Joseph called Barsabas, who was surnamed Justus. . . 4: 36, 9: 36, 10: 5, 12: 12, 13: 1, 13: 9, 15: 22 . . .Paul and Barnabas, namely, Judas, surnamed Barsabbas. . .

> Acts mentions two names to confuse us
> Or maybe he just wanted to amuse us.
> John notes nine surnames
> Was he just playing games?
> Like Barsabbas was a surname of Judas.

Acts 7: 4: Then came he out of the land of the Chaldeans, and dwelt in Haran . Acts. 7: 20: In which time Moses was born, .

> If you don't have the Old Testament
> And you can't find a copy to rent.
> There's a summary in Acts
> With most of the facts
> Which you can easily read during Lent.

Acts 18: 22,23: And when he had landed at Caesarea, and gone up and greeted the church, he went down to Antioch . . .And after he had spent some time there, he departed, and went over all the country of Galatia and Phrygia in order, strengthening all the disciples.

Galatia is one place you could dismiss
Few places are off the highway as this.
Paul wrote to them
As was his system.
Few cities in Asia did he miss.

Acts 20: 35: In all things I have shown you that by so toiling one must help the weak, remembering the words of the Lord Jesus, how he said, "It is more blessed to give than to receive."

We've heard this several times before
So it's something we should not ignore.
To receive is all right,
Even in God's sight,
But it's better to give to the poor.

Acts 28: 1: Where we found brethren, and were desired to tarry with them seven days; and so we went toward Rome.

Acts introduces the reader to Paul
Who helped the Romans heed the call.
After visiting Greece
Did he visit Nice?
It isn't far from Rome, after all.

CHAPTER 4

ROMANS

Romans may not have been the first letter Paul wrote but it is the longest so it is placed first. Paul had never been to Rome but seems to plan to visit that city as well as Spain on some future voyage. There seems to have been a well established Christian colony in Rome and Paul knew, or knew of, several people from that district. His main interests in Romans seem to be circumcision, gays, universal sin, and the duties of Christians. While Romans mentions Paul's travels to Ephesus and Greece he visits Rome only after his letter and then as a prisoner to appeal his case before the Emperor.

Romans 1: 7 : To all that be in Rome, beloved of God, called to be saints: Grace to you and peace from God our Father, and the Lord Jesus Christ.

> Though Paul wrote a letter to Rome
> He longed to leave Israel and roam.
> He wrote down instead
> Everything in his head
> And then had no excuse to leave home.

Romans 1: 13, 15: I wanted you to know, brethren, that I have often intended to come to you . . . in order that I may reap some harvest among you as well as among the rest of the Gentiles . .

so I am eager to preach the gospel to you also who are in Rome.

Paul wrote to Rome to advise them.
He didn't want to surprise 'em.
The letter did reveal
The content of his spiel
And he hoped he might baptize 'em.

Romans 2: 1: Therefore, thou art inexcusable, O man, whosoever thou art that judges; for wherein thou judges another, those condemnest thyself; for thou that judges doest the same things.

Critics were not friends of Paul.
He didn't like judges at all.
As far as he could tell
Judges were guilty as well
Especially if it involved alcohol.

Romans 5: 12-14: Therefore as sin came into the world through one man and death through sin, and so death spread to all men because all men sinned—sin indeed was in the world before the law was given, but sin is not counted where there is no law. Yet death reigned from Adam to Moses.

Augustine wrote about Original Sin
Which Adam and Eve did begin.
Moses brought the law,
Which you previously saw,
Now Heaven, thru Christ, lets you in.

Romans 7: 3: So, then if, while her husband liveth, she be married to another man, she shall be called an adulteress; but if her husband be dead, she is free from that law, . .

If a man should divorce his wife
She must remain single for life.
If the husband be dead
She may then rewed.
What could she do with a knife?

CHAPTER 5

I & II CORINTHIANS

First and Second Corinthians is Paul's attempt to list and correct certain abuses that have been reported to him. Corinth was considered at the time to be a sinful city and the church had been infected. Paul visited Corinth thrice. On his second visit he established the church and stayed over the winter on his last visit.

Paul was disturbed not only by those who associated with fornicators but because there was dissension in the church. It may have been the reason he stayed over the winter in Corinth.

It is reported that Paul's doctrines were victorious and he left the Corinthian church (or churches since most meeting were held in private homes) in much better shape than when he had arrived.

1 Corinthians 3: 6, 12: I have planted, Apollos watered, but God gave the increase. . . Now if any man build on this foundation gold, silver, precious stones, wood, hay, stubble—

> Paul occasionally used metaphor.
> There are probably less than a score.
> Scholars sometimes go crazy

Reading phrases that are hazy.
Thank God Paul didn't use more.

1 Corinthians 6: 16: Do you not know that he who joins himself to a prostitute, becomes one body with her? For as it is written, "The two shall become one."

I suppose a couple should marry
At least they should be rather wary
Just living together
Without a marital tether
Make them One, if only temporary.

1 Corinthians 7: 40: But in my judgment she is happier if she remains as she is.

Did Paul ever have a wife?
He always promoted the single life.
We know all the famous ones,
Priests and the Catholic nuns.
Single people avoid marital strife.

1 Corinthians 10: 32: Give no offense to Jews or to Greeks or to the church of God.

Paul preached among the Greeks.
They were the gentiles that he seeks.
He spent time in Greece
Preaching everlasting peace
And he did this for weeks and for weeks

1 Corinthians 11: 4,5: Any man who prays or prophesies with his head covered dishonors his head, but any woman who prays or prophesies with her head unveiled dishonors her head It is the same as if her head were shaven.

> If you've ever been to Catholic mass
> You'll see that almost every lass
> Wears a white hat
> Or something like that
> And the men? They take a pass.

1 Corinthians 13: 13: So faith, hope, love abide, those three; but the greatest of these is love.

> Faith and Hope we may possess
> And a certain amount of holiness.
> But if love we exhibit
> And hate we prohibit
> We join those that God would bless.

1 Corinthians 14: 5: Now I want you all to speak in tongues, but even more to prophesy. He who prophesies is greater than he who speaks in tongues, unless someone interprets, so that the church may be edified.

> It is recommended that you prophesy
> At least they think you should try.
> Tongues are seldom understood
> And really don't do much good,
> But prophecies are valid, bye and bye.

2 Corinthians 11: 16, 25: I say again, Let no man think me fool; if so, yet as a fool receive me, that I may boast myself a little. . .Thrice I was beaten with rods, once was I stoned, thrice I suffered shipwreck, a night and a day I have been in the deep;

Paul scolds Christians in Corinthians 2.
He also boasts of the perils he knew.
He was imprisoned and stoned
And beaten 'til he moaned
And everything he told them was true.

2 Corinthians 13: 1,2: This is the third time I am coming to you. In the mouth of two or three witnesses shall every word be established. . . I told you before, and tell you beforehand, as if I were present the second time; . . if I come again, I will not spare.

Paul certainly never denied
That he loved traveling worldwide.
Three trips into Greece
Bringing Corinth some peace.
We hope he possessed a Baedeker guide.

GALATIANS, EPHESIANS, PHILIPPIANS, COLOSSIANS, THESSALONIANS, TIMOTHY, TITUS, PHILEMON

Probably because they were so short, many of the epistles were considered 'lesser epistles'. Furthermore, only the first four of these epistles are universally accepted as written by Paul; controversy surrounds many of the others.

Galatians may have been the first of the epistles written by Paul. He visited Galatia, in the middle of Asia Minor, during his first missionary journey, and may have established churches there, though there is no record of that activity.

Ephesians contains words and phrases not found in other letters supposedly written by Paul. Much of his writing was completed in Corinth, or Rome and delivered by one or another of his brothers (or children) in Christ.

Galatians 1: 1,2: Paul, an apostle (not of men, neither by men, but by Jesus Christ, and God the Father, who raised him from the dead;) . . And all the brethren who are with me, unto the churches of Galatia:

There are 21 letters, as I recall.
Only 14 written by Paul.
Were the other seven
Accepted by Heaven
Or were they necessary at all?

Ephesians 1: 1: Paul, an apostle of Jesus Christ by the will of God, to the
saints who are at Ephesus, and to the faithful in Christ Jesus.

For almost two thousand long years
Some scholars have noted their fears.
Paul didn't write Ephesians
For several good reasons
But they didn't convince many peers.

Philippians 1: 3: I thank my God in all my remembrance of you, always
in every prayer of mine for you are making my prayer with joy.

Paul was happy to write Philippians.
They were, to him, ideal Christians.
He was arrested in Rome
Which was his new home,
But he wrote many letters to Grecians.

Colossians 2: 8: See to it that no one makes a prey of you by philosophy
and empty deceit, according to human tradition, . . .

Colossae was nice in its day
But some people started to stray.
Christians became Gnostics,
Paul was more caustic.
Now Colossae looks like Pompei.

1 Thessalonians 1: 2,3 / 3: 10: We give thanks to God always for you all, making mention of you in our prayers, Remembering without ceasing your work of faith, and labor of love, . . .
For even when we were with you, this we commanded you, that if any would not work, neither should he eat.

> Years ago people were self-employed.
> Company jobs very few enjoyed.
> The church's poor box
> Didn't exist or had locks.
> With idleness Paul was annoyed.

1 Timothy 1: 1,2: Paul, an apostle of Christ Jesus by command of God our savior and of Christ Jesus our hope. To Timothy, my true child in the faith:

> Although they are inspired by God
> It still seems rather odd,
> Paul's letters to 'sons'
> Are similar to ones
> That I wrote to my cousin Rod.

1 Timothy 2: 12 : But I permit not a woman to teach, nor to usurp authority over the man, but to be in silence.

> Paul puts women in their place.
> In silence she will surely find grace.
> Eve was easily deceived
> And evidently believed
> Every idea the snake did embrace.

1 Timothy 5: 23: No longer drink only water, but use a little wine for the sake of your stomach and your frequent ailments.

Paul knew the benefits of booze,
T'was wine he was happy to choose.
It's good for the tummy
And some of it's yummy,
Like Manischewitz for the elderly Jews.

1 Timothy 6: 10: For the love of money is the root of all evil, which, while some coveted after, they have erred from the faith, and pierced themselves through with many sorrows.

Is possession of money really bad?
If so that's exceedingly sad.
The word from above
Is that it's the <u>Love</u>
Not the money; aren't you now glad?

Titus 1: 5: This is why I left you in Crete, that you might amend what was defective, and appoint elders in every town as I directed you, . . .

Titus reminds me of Malachi
It's biblical; but nobody knows why.
Some men, I suppose,
Were those that chose
This epistle; or God up on high.

Philemon 1: 1: Paul, a prisoner for Christ Jesus, and Timothy our brother, To Philemon our beloved fellow worker, and Apphia our sister and Archippusn our fellow soldier and the church in your house.

Paul wrote this epistle from Rome.
He was a prisoner in his own home.
So he could write
Even late at night
But he was forbidden to roam

Philemon 1: 10, 24: I beseech thee for my son Onesimus, whom I have begotten in my bonds:. . .Marcus, Aristarchus, Demas, Lucas, my fellow labourers.

Paul's letter to Philemon was to discuss
The relationship of Paul & Onesimus.
Also to ask the man
To do what he can
For Marcus, Demus, and Aristarchus.

CHAPTER 7

HEBREWS

The question of authorship of Hebrews remains to this day. The style is more elegant than the other letters actually written by Paul and a multitude of authors have been suggested over the centuries.

We are not sure to which company of Jews this epistle is addressed; was it to all Jews or to the Jews who had become Christians? There are arguments for both suggestions as well as the idea that the letter speaks to Jewish Christians living in Italy, or more specifically, in Rome.

Leaving those questions aside, we are invited to read of the advantages of the Christian doctrine of salvation through Christ Jesus over the ancient Mosaic laws. Thusly, this letter is addressed to the Jews.

Hebrews 7: 4,5 : See how great he is! Abraham the patriarch gave him a tithe of the spoils. And those descendants of Levi who receive the priestly office have a commandment in the law to take tithes from the people. . .

> Since they no longer made sacrifices
> To priests this caused quite a crisis.
> But they found a way

That then saved the day.
Tithing was one of their devices.

Hebrews 8: 7: For if that first covenant had been faultless, there would have been no occasion for a second.

The covenant with Moses lacked a lot.
Some of that covenant we've forgot.
Now because of Jesus
This new one will please us
It's the one we've fervently sought.

Hebrews 11: 24: By faith Moses, when he was come to years, refused to be called the son of Pharaoh's daughter, Choosing rather to suffer affliction with the people of God than to enjoy the pleasures of sin for a season.

The author of Hebrews was well read
He knew everything Moses had said.
Was he a priest?
An apostle at least.
Or one of the good Lord's appointed?

Hebrews 12: 5: "My son, do not regard lightly the discipline of the Lord, nor lose courage when you are punished by him.

You must have done something bad
To be punished by your Celestial Dad.
God must discipline
Those who commit sin
So accept your fate: don't get mad.

CHAPTER 8

JAMES, PETER 1 & 2, JOHN 1, 2, & 3. JUDE

Because these Epistles are not directed at a specific locale or congregation, such as Corinth or Rome, they are usually listed as 'general' Epistles. James and Peter address their audience as the Christian Jews of the twelve tribes disbursed throughout the world.

These letters are short messages designed to remind the new converts of their rights and responsibilities as Christians. Someone must have found the ten lost tribes in order to convert them from the Laws of Moses to the worship of Jesus Christ.

1 John 2: 9: He who says he is in the light and hates his brother. . . 1 John. 3: 11-12 . . . we should love one another, and not be like Cain who. . .murdered his brother. . . 1 John. 3: 15 Anyone who hates his brother is a murderer. . . . 1 John. 4: 20 If anyone says, "I love God," and hates his brother, he is a liar.

John seems obsessed by some brothers.
Was it his or was it another's?
It's brothers who hate,

That clearly don't rate,
Did a man & John share their mothers?

Jude 1: 14,15: . . . Behold, the Lord cometh. . . to convict all that are ungodly among them of all their ungodly deeds which they have ungodly committed.

Jesus, says Matthew, had 4 brethren.
Were Christ's siblings always men?
Judas "brother Jude"
In a chastising mood
Predicted the ungodly's fate: Amen.

James 5: 2,3: Your riches have rotted and your garments are moth eaten. Your gold and silver have rusted.

James knew few rich he could trust
He felt their gold would soon rust
And while they wait
Their approaching fate
Their garments would all turn to dust

1 Peter 2: 18: Servants, be submissive to your masters
1 Peter 3: 1: Likewise you wives, be submissive to your husbands.

Peter, in his letter, seems to say
That wives and servants should obey
Even if their masters
Are Christian pastors.
Would Peter advise that today?

2 Peter 2: 4: For if God did not spare the angels when they sinned, but cast them into hell and committed them to pits of gloom to be kept until the judgment;

God selected angels as his aids.
They were assigned to different grades.
Some were winners
Others were sinners
And God knew of their escapades.

CHAPTER 9

REVELATION

The last book of the New Testament, written by John, (the apostle, according to some), is an apocalyptic book which includes memories of the past, reports of the present and predictions of the future. While most of us find the book confusing and insensible, certain scholars have studied the writing enough to make sense out of most of it. Therefore the Lamb may signify Christ and the "four horsemen of the apocalypse," war, chaos, famine, and death. Anyone interested may do their own sleuthing and either identify some of the symbols or go crazy trying.

Revelation 6: 4 /19: 19: And there went out another horse that was red; and power was given to him that sat on it to take peace from the earth, . . . And I saw the beast, and the kings of the earth, and their armies, gathered together to make war against him that sat on the horse and against his army.

John, in Revelation, helps us see
The past, the present and what will be.
He saw colored horses
And thousands of forces.
Did John have access to LSD?

Revelation 8: 10: And the third angel sounded, and there fell a great star from heaven, . . .11: 7 . . . the beast that ascendeth out of the bottomless pit shall make war against them.. .and kill them. 12: 7 And there was war in heaven; 13: 7 And it was given unto him to make war with the saints.

John thought meteors were stars.
They certainly were smaller than Mars.
He saw a bottomless pit
With thick smoke in it
And terrestrial, celestial wars.

Revelation 1: 16: . . .In his right hand he held seven stars, from his mouth issued a sharp two-edged sword and his face warlike the sun shining in full strength.

You may think it's rather absurd,
The last book of the Lord God's word.
Sure it seems strange
Like an elephant with mange.
So it's not the book you preferred?

Most of the limericks above are either fair or better but there were some not good enough and were rejected. A small sample of those 41 are printed below. Maybe you consider them better than I did.

Genesis 1: 1:

The name of God you can tell
In Elohim, Ishmael and Israel.
Many years before
On the Euphrates shore
A chief Semite god was called El

Genesis 1: 14:

When finally the fumes went away
And the sun shone brightly all day
On tree and some plants
And beetles and ants
Nobody planned it, some say.

Leviticus 23: 3:

Here's what you can do on Shabbat.
Well, you really can't do a lot.
Take a walk or a nap
And wear a skull-cap
If you work on your car, don't get caught.

Joshua 2: 1,6:

Were Joshua's two spies really lying?
Saying Rahab saved them from dying?
They hid out of sight
And spent the whole night.
But did they do any spying?

Esther 2: 7:

Esther was a young Jewish cutie
Who thought it part of her duty
To change the kings views
So he wouldn't kill Jews.
You can do wonders if you are a beauty.

Jonah 3: 5,11:

Oh to have been a merchant back when
Sackcloth was a main garment back then.
And the king decrees

You must wear one of these
And you sold six score hundred and ten.

Mark 9: 35/ Luke 13:30:

While you were reading Paul's letter
Did you wonder who was the better?
The last shall be first
And that's not the worst
The rich shall wait on the debtor.